Country Roads
~ of ~
MARYLAND
and
DELAWARE

A Guide Book
from Country Roads Press

Country Roads
~ of ~
MARYLAND
and
DELAWARE

W. Lynn Seldon

Illustrated by
Anne Tatgenhorst

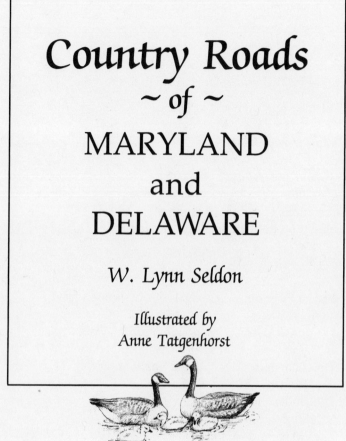

Country Roads Press
CASTINE · MAINE

Country Roads of Maryland and Delaware
© 1994 by W. Lynn Seldon. All rights reserved.

Published by Country Roads Press
P.O. Box 286, Lower Main Street
Castine, Maine 04421

Text and cover design by Edith Allard.
Cover illustration by Victoria Sheridan.
Illustrations by Anne Tatgenhorst.
Typesetting by Camden Type 'n Graphics.

ISBN 1-56626-074-4

Library of Congress Cataloging-in-Publication Data
Seldon, W. Lynn, 1961–
    Country roads of Maryland and Delaware /
W. Lynn Sledon; illustrator, Anne Tatgenhorst with
cover illustration by Victoria Sheridan.
        p.   cm.
    Includes index.
    ISBN 1-56626-074-4 (pbk) : $9.95
    1. Maryland—Guidebooks.   2. Delaware—Guide-
books.   3. Automobile travel—Maryland—Guidebooks.
4. Automobile travel—Delaware—Guidebooks.   I. Title.
F179.3.S45   1994
917.5104'43—dc20   94-7030
                                                    CIP

Printed in the United States of America.
10 9 8 7 6 5 4 3 2 1

To Cele, the Seldon Family, and all
Country Road Lovers

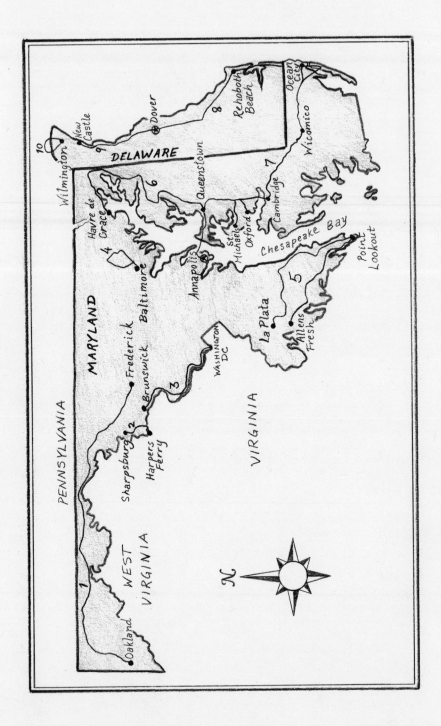

Contents

(& Key to Maryland and Delaware Country Roads)

Introduction

Maryland is definitely the "Land of Pleasant Living," but it is also the land of pleasant driving. Delaware is called a "Small Wonder," and this is especially descriptive for country road drivers looking for lots of mileage from a short country road.

I was born and raised in Virginia and have visited Maryland and Delaware often during my career as a travel writer and photographer. I'm also a big Baltimore Orioles baseball fan and have used them as an excuse for visiting the region frequently.

Preparing this book renewed my immense love for everything these states have to offer. My companion for every mile and word was my soulmate and wife, Cele. When I refer to "we" in the text, you can assume it is the two of us. We've driven more than 5,000 miles in search of perfect country road drives in Maryland and Delaware.

I've chosen a variety of routes to expose readers to the variety of experiences the states offer. Thus, you'll find a country road to pursue almost any special interest you may have.

The interstate system allows you to get to country roads quickly. That means you'll have more time to pursue my recommendations and many of your own discoveries. Allow the time to linger by staying a night or more.

My research and travels for this book put me in contact with some great resources that can help other country road lovers. I highly recommend contacting tourism organizations for information and tips to make your own drives even more enjoyable.

The Maryland Division of Tourism and Promotion (217 East Redwood Street, Baltimore, Maryland 21202, 410-333-6611) is an extremely helpful resource for travel in the state. Liz Barnes and her staff were a great help to me and will be to any readers of this book who contact the office. The individual county tourism offices can also be a helpful source of information to country road drivers.

The Delaware Tourism Office (99 Kings Highway, P.O. Box 1401, Dover, Delaware 19903, 302-739-4271) loves helping country road drivers plan a trip. Stephany Bushweller and the entire tourism office staff are anxious to welcome tourists to this small, wonderful state.

I highly recommend staying in the bed and breakfasts, small inns, and other types of local accommodations throughout both states. There are many excellent books about bed and breakfasts, as well as several organizations to help you find the perfect place to sleep.

Many of the Maryland roads we chose to include are part of the Maryland Scenic Route System. You'll see "Scenic Route" signs, indicated by a black-eyed Susan, the state flower. The scenic route program recognizes certain roads for their historic or scenic interest, and Maryland has lots of history and scenery to see. Though Delaware doesn't have a similar system, the country road drives were easy to choose and even easier to follow.

The state park systems in both states (as well as several national parks) are prevalent along many country roads. Maryland and Delaware have done an excellent job in promoting and preserving the variety of parks.

Along with the above resources, this book could not have been written without the help of many people. Everywhere we went in Maryland and Delaware, we told people about the project, and they did their best to provide information that makes the book better for future visitors.

I would like to thank Margery Read at Country Roads Press for asking me to write this book and supporting the creative process. Nan Smith, my editor, is a writer's best friend. Many of my friends in Virginia, Maryland, and Delaware have contributed some great ideas that made their way into the book. My parents and family contributed a love of this region and support of this travel writing dream that I have somehow made a reality.

My wife, Cele, has been there for me, on the road and at the computer, for the entire project. In many ways, this book is our joint project and a gift of thanks to Maryland and Delaware for having so many wonderful country roads to explore.

MARYLAND

1 ~

The

National

Road

From Baltimore, take I-70 west to Frederick for the start of the drive.

From Washington, D.C., take I-270 north to Frederick for the start of the drive.

Highlights: *Frederick, Hagerstown, many excellent bed and breakfasts, the scenic western Maryland landscape, Cumberland, Grantsville, and Deep Creek Lake. This drive is easily completed in a weekend, but take a few extra days and stay in bed and breakfasts along the way.*

Many people may think that Maryland stops in Frederick and that there's nothing worth visiting west of this historic city. But western Maryland is one of the prettiest and most historic places in the mid-Atlantic area. It's perfect for a few days of country road exploration.

The route taken today by country road drivers is probably the most historic road crossing the Appalachian Mountains. Originally called Nemacolin's Path, it is an old Indian trail, which continued to be used by white settlers and which George Washington traveled many times in his explorations.

The road stretching from Baltimore to Cumberland was commonly called the Baltimore National Pike. The route running from Cumberland all the way to Vandalia, Illinois, was referred to as the Cumberland Road and the National Road, which was America's first federally funded highway, authorized by Congress in 1806. The entire Maryland stretch from Baltimore is now called the National Freeway, but most of the best country road sections lie west of Frederick.

It's best to take I-70 or I-270 directly to Frederick, with a stopover in New Market if you have time. New Market somehow remains an idyllic small town. Main Street is perfect for sidewalk strolling and antique shopping (the town is one of Maryland's main antiques meccas).

If you've started this drive late in the day, New Market (or Frederick) is a great place to spend the night. The Strawberry Inn, right on Main Street, is a fully restored 1837 farmhouse, with five guest rooms furnished with antiques. Jane and Ed Rossig are very welcoming New Market hosts. Ask them about dinner at Mealey's Restaurant, the Yates Market and Hardware Store, the New Market General Store, and any secrets they will share about shopping for antiques.

Just eight miles west, Frederick provides a historical introduction to another Maryland. With an ever-expanding population of 50,000, Frederick is nationally recognized for its thirty-three-block historic district. The downtown area features stately and historic architecture, fine dining, and wonderful shopping and antiquing possibilities.

Follow the signs into the town center's visitors center for the start of a walking and driving tour. The helpful staff can provide information about guided tours, carriage rides, and sightseeing. Big-city dwellers will find western Maryland hospitality refreshing.

4

Frederick is simply steeped in history. Founded in 1745 by English and German settlers as Fredericktown, it served at that time as a frontier town for wagon trains making the first trips across the Allegheny Mountains. While pioneers passed through town first, Abraham Lincoln came later to address the citizens after the Battle of Antietam (see Chapter 2).

The city's star-spangled natives include Francis Scott Key (author of the national anthem), Chief Justice Roger Brooke Taney (whose Dred Scott decision ultimately led to the Emancipation Proclamation), and Barbara Fritchie (who publicly defied Stonewall Jackson and his troops by flying the American flag). Today, much of this history can still be explored.

You will enjoy the walking tour as much or more than the scenic drive. Historic highlights include the Historical Society and Museum, St. John the Evangelist Roman Catholic Church (America's oldest consecrated Catholic church), the carriage house and slave quarters of the Ross/Mathias mansions, Old City Hall, the law offices of Roger Brooke Taney and Francis Scott Key (brothers-in-law who practiced law together), and dozens of beautiful old buildings of historical significance.

The renovated downtown area also offers lots of shopping and dining possibilities. Some dining favorites we found were Brown Pelican, The Province, the Starving Artist Cafe, and Tauraso's/Victor's Saloon and Raw Bar. Unique specialty shopping possibilities include Carriage Trade, Country Wares of Frederick, Flights of Fancy, and many antique shops.

The driving tour around the city isn't exactly a country road drive, but it once was and still offers a glimpse of Frederick's countryside. With so many interesting places, this tour could take an entire day. Be prepared for lots of stops if you're a history buff.

Required car stops should be the Schifferstadt Architectural Museum, the grave of U.S. Supreme Court Chief Justice Roger Brooke Taney, Everedy Square and Shab Row (restored eighteenth- and nineteenth-century dwellings), the Barbara

" 'Shoot if you must this old grey head
But spare your country's flag,' she said."
Whittier's poem made Barbara Fritchie's defiance of
Stonewall Jackson a legend

Fritchie Replica House and Museum, the Roger Brooke Taney House and Francis Scott Key Museum, the Mount Olivet Cemetery (Barbara Fritchie's grave and the Francis Scott Key Monument), the old Baltimore and Ohio Railroad Station (site of Abraham Lincoln's Antietam speech), and the Civil War's Monocacy National Battlefield.

North of town, Frederick County features a number of covered bridges. Just off US 15, Loy's Station (1850), Roddy

Road (1856), and Utica (1850) all provide delightful examples of old country road landmarks, including the covered bridge.

If, after all this walking and driving, you want to spend the night in Frederick before heading farther west, you will find that the town has some nice small lodging options.

One local favorite is the Tyler-Spite House, conveniently located in the heart of Frederick's historic district. This elegantly restored three-story Federal-style mansion, located on Courthouse Square, was built by Dr. John Tyler in 1814. The owners offer six beautifully appointed rooms, carriage rides, a gourmet breakfast, and afternoon tea. Inns of the Blue Ridge, an excellent accommodations service, is also based in Frederick.

Frederick is just the beginning of western Maryland, and although driving west on US 40 takes you through areas of suburban commercialism, there are many lovely country roads to come. US 40 leads right into Hagerstown, a town first settled by German immigrant Jonathan Hager in 1739, and which still retains many historic buildings. These include the Miller House (a typical townhouse built in the 1820s), the Valley Store Museum, and the Hager House and Museum—all worthwhile visits.

Just outside the downtown area is the Rose Hill Cemetery. This pretty place features a monument to Thomas Kennedy, a local merchant who spent almost twenty years fighting for Jews to have the same rights enjoyed by other citizens (the Jew Bill was passed in 1826). Washington Cemetery, located within Rose Hill, is dedicated to the Confederate soldiers who died at Antietam and South Mountain.

Hagerstown has a real German feel to it, which is enhanced by the Schmankerl Stube Bavarian Restaurant. It's a little bit of Germany in western Maryland. Charlie Sekula, a native of Bavaria, is the owner and frequent host of this wonderful restaurant and bar. The ethnic atmosphere is authentic, with waiters dressed in traditional costumes and a strolling accordionist on the weekends. There's even a "biergarten" out back for warm weather. The bar features several great German beers on draft (Hacker Pschorr and Weissbier are notable), as well as many more bottled choices. The German cuisine, prepared by Bavarian chefs Klaus and Hans, is tasty and filling. It's the perfect place to experience the ethnicity that pervades much of western Maryland.

Back on US 40, just west of Hagerstown is the wonderful Wilson complex. Many drivers who stop for a look end up spending the night, and for good reason: The Wilson complex is made up of the Wilson House bed and breakfast, Wilson's General Store, and Wilson's School. You will feel like you've stopped in the 1850s.

Rufus Wilson moved to Washington County in 1847 and established this popular general store. Lewis and Francis Horst restored it in 1984, and it now operates and looks much like it did in the 1850s. Visitors can enjoy eating loose candy, home-baked goods, meats, and sharp cheese, playing a game of checkers by the woodstove, and looking at many of the store's varied original items. Upstairs, there's an emporium selling updated traditional clothing for women.

Next to the store sits Wilson's School, which was built in 1855 by Rufus Wilson for the education of his son John. The Horsts purchased the school in 1987 and restored it to its original state, complete with antique wooden desks, old books, lunch pails, and vintage clothes hanging in the small cloakroom. You can almost see a little child sitting in the corner with a dunce cap in place.

The Wilson House bed and breakfast completes the feeling of being in an 1850s time machine. This newly restored country home, built by Rufus Wilson in 1850, now features large rooms overlooking the picturesque countryside. The

large bedrooms and the rest of the house are filled with historical antiques and stories, completing this fascinating trip back
to the 1850s. Guests are treated to a huge country breakfast
each morning.

Back on US 40, it's Westward ho! once again. The elevation begins to increase as you drive into the mountains and
begin to see spectacular views ahead. US 40 becomes I-70 for
the last ten miles into Hancock. Hancock is worth a stop to
visit the Chesapeake and Ohio Canal Visitor Center, which
provides an excellent introduction to the canal and a convenient chance to hike some of the trail (see Chapter 3).

US 40 weaves its way out of Hancock and over five
mountains to Cumberland. The overlooks at Martin's Mountain (1,695 feet), Polish Mountain (1,340 feet), Green Ridge
(1,575 feet), Town Hill (1,600 feet), and Sideline Hill (1,575
feet) are all easy and pretty pulloffs.

Historic Cumberland provides a great place to stop for
the day or a night. A tourism office, located in the Western
Maryland Station, can provide maps, walking tour information, and recommendations for restaurants and accommodations. Upstairs in this train depot, which was built in 1913,
train buffs find interesting memorabilia and exhibits, as well
as the end of the C&O Canal National Historical Park. Steam
train tours of the area are also offered by the Western Maryland Scenic Railroad.

The town of Cumberland is a great place for a walk into
the past. The Washington Street Historic District, located on a
steep hill, features many renovated houses and buildings.
Some of the most famous are Emmanuel Episcopal Church,
the Allegheny Court House, and History House, home of the
Allegheny County Historical Society.

Greene Street runs parallel to Washington Street and features Riverside Park, which contains the site of one of George Washington's headquarters and the Thomas Cresap Memorial. Washington used this small log cabin as his base during the French and Indian Wars and the Whiskey Rebellion. The memorial for Thomas Cresap pays tribute to the famous pioneer who was a trailblazer west of the Alleghenies.

Back in the center of town, two meccas are hard to ignore, because of the smells wafting down North Liberty Street. Coney Island and Curtis's have been serving "famous wieners" since 1918. The tasty hot dogs and atmosphere are local legends and so are the friendly family members who run the restaurants. The business was originally known as Coney Island Lunch. Louis, Alcea (D'Ascenzo), and L. Gino Giatras have carried on the tradition with these two locations. Louis and Alcea's three sons, Anthony, Troy, and Gino, are now involved in the business, and Gino will eventually be in charge of both operations. Either restaurant offers a good opportunity to meet friendly locals and enjoy an unusual meal.

Cumberland is also a perfect place for the night, and you might choose to spend it at The Inn at Walnut Bottom. Well situated at 120 Greene Street, this quaint inn features twelve unique rooms and the hospitality of innkeeper Sharon Ennis Kazary, her husband Robert, and their children William and Ellen. Next door to the inn, the Oxford House Restaurant, hosted by Jaye and Bill Miller, offers homemade and traditional country fare. A full country inn breakfast (at the Oxford House) awaits country road drivers in the morning.

Just west of Cumberland, on the road to Frostburg (Alternate US 40), you will pass through "the Narrows," a famous 1,000-foot-wide gap in Wills Mountain. Originally known as "the Gateway of the West," it provides a convenient route

Church spires in Cumberland

westward. The view from below and above at Lover's Leap can be awe-inspiring.

Frostburg is the western terminus for the Western Maryland Scenic Railroad (see the Cumberland section), situated in an 1891 renovated train station, which features the railroad-themed Old Depot restaurant, a bakery, ice cream parlor, and lounge. Many of the homes along Main Street were built during the early National Road days. Hotel buffs should check out Failingers Hotel Gunter, a grand old restored 1896 hotel at 11 West Main Street.

Continue to drive west on Alternate US 40 out of Frostburg, over Big Savage Mountain (elevation 2,850 feet), and toward the interesting town of Grantsville in Garrett County. The first stop in Grantsville has to be the Casselman Hotel.

This historic hotel was built in 1824 by Solomon Sterner as a hostelry to serve travelers on the National Road. It has been known at various times as Sterner's Tavern, Drover's Inn, Farmer's Hotel, Dorsey's Hotel, and finally as the Casselman Hotel. The large Federal-style brick building features fireplaces in every room (used for both heating and cooking) and beautiful woodwork throughout.

The current owners, the friendly Miller family, acquired the hotel in 1964 and have added a new dining room and the popular forty-room motor inn. The main building offers five varied bed-and-breakfast-style rooms, so that visitors are able to live in history for the night. In the dining room, a popular destination for guests, the fare is simple country food, with a variety of interesting Amish recipes served by Amish locals. The downstairs bakery turns out tasty breads, cakes, and pies for the restaurant and tantalizing take-home purchases for travelers.

Just down the road sits Penn Alps, a once busy stagecoach stop that now attracts crafts shoppers as well as diners.

The crafts shop features a large selection of work from local craftspeople. Outside the shop, crafts demonstrations are featured in several log huts.

Penn Alps is a great place to park so that you can view the Casselman Bridge, a huge stone bridge built in 1813 that was the longest single-span bridge in the United States (eighty feet). It once provided a link between Cumberland and Wheeling, West Virginia, but it is now closed. It remains a picturesque and nostalgic reminder of country roads past.

Just west of Grantsville on Alternate US 40, turn right onto US 669 and look for Yoder Country Market on the right. This unusual supermarket began as a butcher shop on the Yoders' Mennonite family farm in 1947. The market is famed for its bologna, sausages, smoked ham, canned meats, fresh-baked breads, handmade Amish noodles, and many other delicacies.

Take Alternate US 40 out of Grantsville to Keysers Ridge and then left onto US 219, the road to Deep Creek Lake. Plan to stay a bit once you get there.

Deep Creek Lake is another Maryland gem hidden down another country road. Set amidst the mountains of Garrett County, Maryland's largest freshwater lake is twelve miles long and offers sixty-five miles of shoreline. On warm days, the lake is popular for boating, water sports, and golf. In the winter, Wisp Ski Resort offers more than twelve miles of slopes and trails.

The four-season resort is an ideal western Maryland driving destination and has become a major outdoor recreation and tourist center. Accommodations for visitors include many lakeside resorts, hotels, condominiums, and houses that are for rent year-round. The nearby Harley Farm offers bed and breakfast accommodations on a sixty-five-acre farm, and you will enjoy the local hospitality and experience of the Gillespies as your hosts.

Along with all the amenities of Deep Creek Lake, Harley Farm affords the opportunity to wander around an active farm and down many country lanes. You'll return to a modern room, a casual sitting area, and a huge, creatively prepared breakfast in the morning. If they're full, try Red Run Inn nearby.

Besides beautiful drives around the lake and through the mountainous countryside, there's much to see and do in the Deep Creek Lake area. Skiing, boating, and other water sports are easy to arrange. Additional recreational activities include fishing, swimming, hiking, biking, horseback riding, shopping, and snowmobiling.

As with many resort areas, dining is the primary evening passion. Some local recommendations include Silver Tree Restaurant (Italian food and a casual, upbeat lakeside atmosphere), McClive's Restaurant and Lounge (lakeside), and Doctor Willy's Great American Seafood Company.

Oakland, the county seat, is the last stop in this western Maryland odyssey. This historic and lovely town is just eight miles south of Deep Creek Lake on US 219.

An old railroad town, Oakland features many historic houses and lots of small-town charm. Railroad buffs will definitely want to take cameras along to take pictures of the old Queen Anne–style B&O Railroad Station. If this is the end of the road for the day, make sure to stay at the Oak and Apple and to enjoy a meal at the Cornish Manor.

The area around Oakland is famous for many outdoor scenic and recreational opportunities. Muddy Creek Falls, Garrett State Forest, Cranesville Swamp, and Backbone Mountain (3,360 feet, the highest point in Maryland) are some of the most popular destinations.

In the Area

Strawberry Inn (New Market): 301-865-3318

Mealey's Restaurant (New Market): 301-865-5488

Frederick Visitor Center (Frederick): 301-663-8687 or 800-999-3613

Brown Pelican (Frederick): 301-695-5833

The Province (Frederick): 301-663-1441

Starving Artist Cafe (Frederick): 301-663-0073

Tauraso's/Victor's Saloon and Raw Bar (Frederick): 301-663-6600

Carriage Trade (Frederick): 301-662-1411

Country Wares of Frederick (Frederick): 301-694-0990

Flights of Fancy (Frederick): 301-663-9295

Museum Shop, Ltd. (Frederick): 301-695-0424

Tyler-Spite House (Frederick): 301-831-4455

Inns of the Blue Ridge (Frederick): 301-694-0440

Schmankerl Stube Bavarian Restaurant (Hagerstown): 301-797-3354

Wilson House Bed and Breakfast (Wilson): 301-582-4320

Chesapeake and Ohio Canal Visitor Center (Hancock): 301-678-5463

Western Maryland Scenic Railroad (Cumberland): 301-759-4400

Coney Island and Curtis's (Cumberland): 301-777-9707

The Inn at Walnut Bottom (Cumberland): 301-777-0003

The Oxford House Restaurant (Cumberland): 301-777-7101

Casselman Hotel (Grantsville): 301-895-5055

Penn Alps (Grantsville): 301-895-5985

Yoder Country Market (Grantsville): 301-895-5148
Wisp Ski Resort (McHenry): 301-387-4911
Harley Farm (Deep Creek Lake): 301-387-9050
Red Run Inn (Deep Creek Lake): 301-387-9050
Oak and Apple (Oakland): 301-334-9265
Cornish Manor (Oakland): 301-334-3551

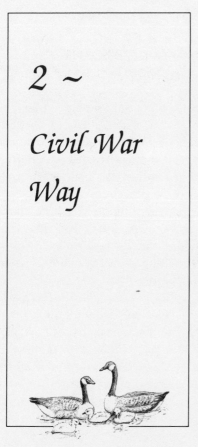

2 ~

Civil War

Way

From Baltimore, take I-70 west to Frederick and then US 340 west to Harpers Ferry, West Virginia, for the start of the drive. If you want to skip Harpers Ferry and head straight to Antietam, take State 67 toward Boonsboro and Sharpsburg.

From Washington, D.C., take I-270 north to Frederick and then US 340 west to Harpers Ferry, West Virginia, for the start of the drive. If you want to skip Harpers Ferry and head straight to Antietam, take State 67 north toward Boonsboro and Sharpsburg.

Highlights: *Harpers Ferry, rolling Washington County countryside, Sharpsburg, and the Antietam National Battlefield. This drive is easily completed in a day, but take a weekend and stay in a bed and breakfast.*

The Civil War means much to Marylanders and those who visit the state. The Mason-Dixon line divided Maryland and Pennsylvania, as well as a nation. Many Civil War battles were fought on Maryland soil, and much of this history can still be explored today.

The best place to start a Maryland Civil War drive isn't even in the state. Head across the Potomac to Harpers Ferry National Historical Park in West Virginia for a well-preserved and well-presented look at another era.

It's best to follow the signs to the official park entrance and park there, rather than trying to find a rare parking space in Harpers Ferry itself. Helpful visitors center personnel can answer questions, provide maps, and get you on the frequent shuttle into town.

This modern bus deposits you back into time in another world. Situated at the confluence of the Shenandoah and Potomac Rivers in the shadow of the Blue Ridge Mountains, Harpers Ferry became an important industrialized transportation hub and arms-producing town in the eighteenth and nineteenth centuries.

Harpers Ferry came to national prominence on the night of October 16, 1859, with John Brown's infamous raid. John Brown was a staunch abolitionist who devised a plan to liberate slaves through violence, setting up a stronghold in the mountains of Maryland and Virginia.

Starting his operation with an insurrection in Harpers Ferry, Brown had chosen the town for its location near the Mason-Dixon line, easy access to the mountains for guerrilla warfare, and the proximity of a large stock of arms. Brown and his twenty-one-man army seized the armory and other strategic points before the townspeople could react.

The militia of Harpers Ferry finally cornered Brown and his men in the armory/fire engine-house/guardhouse (now called "John Brown's Fort"). They were captured on the morning of October 18 by a contingent of marines led by Col. Robert E. Lee and Lieut. J.E.B. Stuart.

John Brown was tried for murder, treason, and conspiracy with slaves to create insurrection. He was found guilty and hanged in Charles Town on December 2, 1859.

On that day, Brown wrote a prophetic note to the nation: "I, John Brown, am now quite certain that the crimes of this guilty land will never be purged away but with blood. I had, as I now think, vainly flattered myself that without very much bloodshed it might be done." The Civil War started a short sixteen months later on April 12, 1861, at Fort Sumter in Charleston, South Carolina.

Harpers Ferry was devastated during the Civil War. Because of its strategic location, the town was occupied by both sides and suffered through many major battles. The armory and arsenal buildings were intentionally destroyed by fire in 1861 to keep them from being captured by Confederate troops.

Many people left the war-ravaged town, which went through additional damage from a series of serious floods in the late 1800s. It fell into decay before serious restoration work by the government later saved the town for future generations of visitors.

Today, Harpers Ferry National Historical Park is a national treasure. The shuttle bus deposits visitors in the middle of a group of restored historic buildings, exhibits, shops, and restaurants.

The park map will guide you on an extensive walking tour, which starts in the information center housed in the old Stagecoach Inn, run by Maj. James Stephenson from 1826 to 1834.

Along Shenandoah Street, many buildings evoke the boom days of Harpers Ferry. The re-created Provost Office shows the wartime office of the Union provost guard. The Dry Goods Store, built in 1812, depicts a typical dry goods store of the 1850s. Next door the Master Armorer's House serves as a fascinating museum that demonstrates the history of gunmaking.

Farther down Shenandoah Street, the John Brown Museum houses a theater and a museum that relates the events of John Brown's historic raid. Across the street, John Brown's Fort has been restored. Behind the fort, you will have a great scenic view of Maryland and Virginia across the rivers.

St. Peter's Catholic Church looms over the landscape of Harpers Ferry. Hearty walkers can make their way up the stone steps (cut into natural rock in the 1800s) to the lovely 1830s church. Even farther up you will find Jefferson Rock, which offers a view that Thomas Jefferson said was "worth a voyage across the Atlantic."

Back in town, High Street and Potomac Street offer more museums, shops, and restaurants. We particularly enjoyed the Civil War museums and the Black history exhibit.

Harpers Ferry is also conveniently close to the C&O Canal National Historical Park (see Chapter 3) and the Appalachian Trail. The Appalachian National Scenic Trail is one of the world's greatest hiking trails. The famed A.T. is a 2,144-mile hiking "path" along the ridge of the Appalachian Mountains. Beginning in Georgia, it runs through fourteen states to its terminus at Mt. Katahdin, in Maine.

The first section of the A.T. was constructed in New Jersey in 1922. The Appalachian Mountain Club became involved in its development, as did individuals like Benton MacKaye, Arthur Perkins, and Myron H. Avery. With the help of the Civilian Conservation Corps, many hiking clubs, and thousands of other volunteers, all sections of the A.T. were finally relocated, opened, and marked for hikers and outdoors lovers in 1951.

In 1968, the National Trails Systems Act made the A.T. a linear national park and authorized funds to surround the entire route with public lands. The A.T. is now maintained by a variety of active local clubs and government agencies. The Appalachian Trail Conference, based in Harpers Ferry, is in constant need of ecotourist volunteers all along the A.T.

The Appalachian Trail serves as a great retreat from eastern urban life—more than two-thirds of the nation's population lives within 550 miles of it. Due to the A.T. headquarters' location, Harpers Ferry is a mecca for many hikers. Contact the Appalachian Trail Conference at P.O. Box 807, Harpers Ferry, West Virginia 25425 (304-535-6331).

Follow US 340 out of Harpers Ferry, across the Potomac, and into Maryland. Take a left onto State 67 toward Boonsboro and Sharpsburg.

This modern highway belies the battle that took place just ahead. Take State 67 to Boonsboro and then turn left onto State 34 for Sharpsburg, a charming small town worth further exploration after heading north on State 65 to the Antietam National Battlefield.

The large visitors center provides an excellent driving map, helpful information, an audiovisual program, and a sweeping view of part of the battlefield. The driving tour is simply one of the most sobering and interesting short country road drives in America.

The Burnside Bridge at Antietam

The drive should take about two hours, but it could take much longer, depending on your depth of interest in the Civil War. There are many fascinating pulloffs, displays, and remnants of the battle along the route.

The Battle of Antietam on September 17, 1862, was the climax of Gen. Robert E. Lee's first attempt at carrying the Civil War into Northern territory. Lee's Confederate force of 41,000 fought the 87,000 troops of the Federal Army of the Potomac under Gen. George B. McClellan. By the end of the battle, the course of the Civil War was greatly changed.

By September 15, battle lines had been established by the two forces on each side of Antietam Creek near the town of Sharpsburg. The arrival of additional troops with Confederate Gen. Thomas "Stonewall" Jackson on September 16 set the stage for a big battle. The driving tour follows the stages of the battle.

The fighting opened at dawn on September 17, with Union Gen. Joseph Hooker sending a barrage of fire on Jackson's men. Of the opening, he reported, "In the time I am writing, every stalk of corn in the northern and greater part of the field was cut as closely as could have been done with a knife, and the slain lay in rows precisely as they had stood in their ranks a few moments before."

The drive leads through the North Woods, where Hooker launched the attack. He was stopped by Jackson's troops in the Cornfield, just down the road. In the West Woods a bit later, Union forces lost more than 2,200 men in less than half an hour.

The drive leads past Mumma Farm, which was burned by the Confederates to keep Union sharpshooters from using it. The structures at the farm were the only civilian buildings purposely destroyed during the fighting.

Union forces moved through Roulette Farm to further the attack on the Confederates posted along the old sunken road. Bitter fighting raged along this road for almost four hours, resulting in about 4,000 casualties and the name "Bloody Lane."

Union Gen. Ambrose E. Burnside was having trouble crossing the Lower Bridge over Antietam Creek. About 400 Georgia Confederates used their high-ground position to hold off the larger contingent under General Burnside. Union troops finally crossed the bridge, driving the Confederates near Sharpsburg, before Gen. A. P. Hill's Confederate division arrived from Harpers Ferry and saved the day.

General Hill and his troops arrived just as darkness came. This enabled Lee's troops to regroup, and he withdrew his army across the Potomac the next day. Though neither side could claim clear victory, this bloody battle and Lee's failure to carry the war into the North caused Great Britain to postpone recognition of the Confederate government and gave President Abraham Lincoln the opportunity to issue the Emancipation Proclamation.

Our country drive ends at Antietam National Cemetery. More men were probably killed or wounded at Antietam on September 17, 1862, than on any other single day in the Civil War. Union losses totaled 12,410, and Confederate losses reached about 10,700. The cemetery contains the graves of 4,776 Federal soldiers, including 1,836 who are unknown. Most of the Confederate dead were buried in Hagerstown and Frederick, as well as in Shepherdstown, West Virginia, and in many local church and family cemeteries.

The best way to end this historic drive and the day is by staying at an appropriate bed and breakfast. Our favorite choice, if they have room, is the Inn at Antietam. Situated right on Main Street in Sharpsburg, this lovely white country Victorian house features antique-filled rooms, a huge porch, a convenient location, and the wonderful hospitality of the Fairbourns. Besides their big breakfasts, the Fairbourns can make recommendations for meals at other restaurants in the area.

If the Inn at Antietam is full, try any of the following: Antietam Overlook Farm Bed and Breakfast, Ground Squirrel Holler, the Jacob Rohrbach Inn, or the Piper House. As with the Antietam National Battlefield, they all offer an inside look at history. It's a great way to end the drive.

In the Area

Harpers Ferry National Historical Park (Harpers Ferry): 304-535-6371

Appalachian Trail Conference (Harpers Ferry): 304-535-6331

Antietam National Battlefield (Sharpsburg): 301-432-5124

Inn at Antietam (Sharpsburg): 301-432-6601

Antietam Overlook Farm Bed and Breakfast (Keedysville): 800-878-4241

Ground Squirrel Holler (Sharpsburg): 301-432-8288

Jacob Rohrbach Inn (Sharpsburg): 301-432-5079

Piper House (Sharpsburg): 301-797-1862

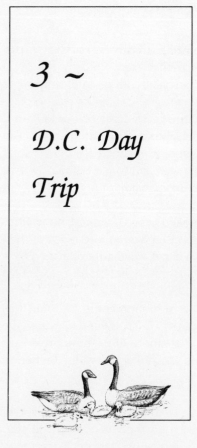

3 ~

D.C. Day

Trip

From Washington, D.C., take the Beltway (I-495) out to the Great Falls exit (MacArthur Boulevard). Follow the signs toward Great Falls for the start of the drive.

Highlights: *Old Angler's Inn, the Chesapeake and Ohio Canal National Historical Park, Great Falls, and Brunswick. This drive is easily completed in a day.*

As you leave the busy highways of Washington, D.C., it's hard to believe that a peaceful country road is just outside the Beltway. But traffic jams are left far behind when you hit MacArthur Boulevard and the road to (and beyond) Great Falls.

This country road runs roughly parallel with the Chesapeake and Ohio Canal, which stretches beside the Potomac River from the mouth of Rock Creek in Georgetown all the way to Cumberland, Maryland (184.5 miles). Its seventy-four lift locks raise the canal from near sea level to an elevation of 605 feet in Cumberland. Its towpath has become a haven for hikers, cyclists, and country road drivers escaping urban and suburban life. Other activities supported by the canal include canoeing, fishing, horseback riding, and camping at its many campsites.

George Washington originally thought of the idea of a waterway connecting the Chesapeake Bay with the Ohio Valley. His plans led to the design and construction of a long canal system. By 1802, canals were cut to get around the five falls of the Potomac River, but expansion of the canal did not occur until the mid-1800s.

By the time the C&O Canal reached Cumberland in 1850, trains had already shown that they were more efficient than the barges on the canal. The canal was badly damaged by a flood in 1889 and by another one in 1924, and commercial barge traffic came to a halt.

The canal became a national monument in 1961 and was named a national historical park in 1971. It winds through the Piedmont on the Allegheny Plateau, right past the Great Falls of the Potomac, and through the ridge and valley section of the Appalachian Mountains.

The zero milepost of the canal is actually at the Georgetown Visitor Center. However, it's more convenient to start the drive outside the Beltway. If you do start in Georgetown, take M Street out to MacArthur Boulevard and Canal Road. The sights and scenes along the way are a great warm-up for Great Falls.

Outside I-495, MacArthur Boulevard is far from the madding crowds and cars as it winds its way toward Great Falls. Try to time your departure so that you're hungry when you start the drive (before Sunday brunch or before dinner any evening is ideal). Your first stop should be the Old Angler's Inn. You can't miss it on the right, about five miles past I-495.

Along the towpath of the C&O Canal

Since 1860, the Old Angler's Inn has been serving country road drivers. Near this site, the Indians of the Algonquin Nation maintained a post for their "traveling traders," after whom the Patauomeck River was named. In the summer of 1608, Capt. John Smith made camp nearby on his canoe trip up the Potomac.

Construction of the C&O Canal began in 1828, and the Old Angler's Inn was opened in 1860 to serve those journeying to and from the nation's capital, as well as residents of the city and countryside nearby. It still does so today.

The inn served as a resting place for soldiers during the Civil War, as officers and men from both sides stopped there for the night. Later, Teddy Roosevelt used the inn as a base of operations for his hunting and fishing expeditions.

After a beautiful restoration in 1937, the Old Angler's Inn has become a great place to stop before or after a day in the country. It's well worth it to time your stop to enjoy a nice meal there.

The Old Angler's Inn puts you in a peaceful mood for visiting Great Falls. The Great Falls of the Potomac River have been attracting visitors since the early days of the C&O Canal. The Great Falls Tavern was first built as a lockhouse and had to be expanded twice in its first four years.

The overlooks on the Potomac are quite beautiful, so don't forget your camera. The day-hike opportunities are excellent. A few of our favorites include Gold Mine Loop (4.2 miles), Berma Road (3.3-mile loop to Angler's Inn), and the Billy Goat Trail (4 miles).

The tavern visitors center includes exhibits (the lock model is interesting), canal-era artifacts, books, and well-informed people. A snack bar is also open from April through October.

You could easily spend an entire day in the Great Falls area, but the rest of this country road drive is just as interesting. Take State 189 north to the intersection with State 190 and make a left turn (River Road). This stretch runs through several suburban developments and some very expensive real estate. Soon, however, any memories of suburbia are quickly forgotten.

This part of the drive requires a few turns and a map, but it's worth the effort. State 190 runs into Seneca Creek State Park and State 112. This wild park features 5,000 acres of woods, streams, and lots of fauna and flora. Within the park, the 500-acre Clopper area is the only developed portion, making it ideal for picnics, hiking, and biking.

Take State 112 north for a short distance before turning left onto State 107 going west toward Poolesville. This historic town was settled by John Poole in the late 1700s and grew as the C&O Canal and the farming economy grew in the area. Many nineteenth-century homes can be seen as you drive through Poolesville. You can even obtain a map at the town hall.

Take State 107 out to the river (White's Ferry Road) to White's Ferry, the only remaining operational ferry on the Potomac River. Also nearby, the Seneca Schoolhouse, a one-room school built of Seneca sandstone in 1866, is now an interesting museum.

After a brief stay in Poolesville, head north on State 109 toward Beallsville and travel through some beautiful farmland. This road parallels the Potomac all the way to Point of Rocks.

The highway crosses over the Monocacy Scenic River (the canal's impressive stone Monocacy Aqueduct is the longest on the river) and into Frederick County. It winds through eye-pleasing farmland and into Point of Rocks. The handsome Victorian Point of Rocks Railroad Station, built in the late 1800s, is still used today.

You have to take US 15 north toward Frederick for a few miles before turning onto quiet State 464 toward Brunswick. The hilly town of Brunswick (originally called Berlin) was an important river crossing point and rail depot during the Civil War and was also a railroad boomtown. It's a nice place to get out and stretch your legs.

The Brunswick Museum at 40 West Potomac Street is fascinating. It concentrates on the influence of the railroad and C&O Canal, with many artifacts from throughout this quaint town's history. Railroad buffs should also stop by the Old B&O Roundhouse, where train engines change directions. The old railroad station is also still in use.

Antique lovers will definitely want to visit Gunther's International Auction Gallery at 24 South Virginia Avenue. This popular spot has hundreds of antiques and collectibles in a relaxed shopping atmosphere.

Dining and overnight accommodations are limited in Brunswick, and you are better off heading to Harpers Ferry, West Virginia, or Frederick for the night.

State 478 leads out to US 340 and the end of the drive. It's easiest to return to Washington, D.C., by way of US 340 to Frederick and then to I-270. Another option is to explore Harpers Ferry or to continue on for some Civil War history around Sharpsburg (Chapter 2).

In the Area

Chesapeake and Ohio Canal National Historical Park
(Great Falls): 301-739-4200

Old Angler's Inn (Potomac): 301-365-2425

Poolesville Town Hall (Poolesville): 301-428-8927

White's Ferry (Poolesville): 301-349-5200

Seneca Schoolhouse (Poolesville): 301-972-8588

Brunswick Museum (Brunswick): 301-834-7100

Gunther's International Auction Gallery (Brunswick):
301-663-0406

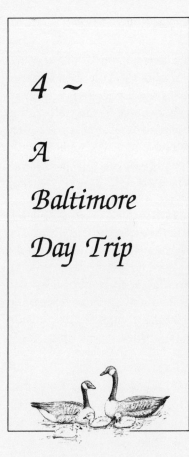

4 ~

A

Baltimore

Day Trip

From Baltimore, take State 45 out of downtown for the start of the drive at State 146 in Towson.

Highlights: *Towson Town Center, Loch Raven Reservoir, Ladew Topiary Gardens, Rocks State Park, Bel Air, and Gunpowder Falls State Park. This drive is easily completed in a day.*

Fast-paced living in Baltimore is easily left behind in just a few miles of driving. The country surrounding the city is packed with things to see and do down quiet and slow-paced country roads.

North of Baltimore, drivers can find rolling countryside, small towns, and much to see in the great outdoors. It's just a short drive out Greenmount Avenue and York Road (State 45) to Towson and a world away from Baltimore.

Historic Towson, the county seat, suffers from a bit of Baltimore suburban sprawl. However, some highlights include

Towson Town Center (one of the largest malls in America), the Sheppard-Pratt Hospital Buildings (c. 1862) on North Charles Street, and the house on Osler Drive where F. Scott Fitzgerald stayed when Zelda was at St. Joseph's Hospital. Eating options are limited on this drive, and Towson is a great place to purchase food to make a picnic later.

Heading out of Towson on State 146, the road quickly turns into a two-lane country road. On the right, the Hampton National Historic Site, at 523 Hampton Lane, is a classic example of a U.S. mansion constructed in the late 1700s. The huge estate was built by Charles Ridgely, owner of the Northampton Ironworks (supplier for the Continental Army during the Revolutionary War). The elegant old house and grounds provide a beautiful setting for guided tours and relaxed wandering. There are twenty-seven buildings, including the mansion, slave quarters, stables, a gift shop, and a tearoom (lunch available).

State 146 passes right over Loch Raven Reservoir. This large body of water is ten miles long, with 2,400 acres of water and 5,600 acres of protected land. The park features picnic areas, hiking, fishing, and boat rentals.

The winding road then leads through farmland, past large farmhouses, horse pastures, and plantations as you drive into Harford County. Ladew Topiary Gardens, only fifteen miles north of Baltimore, is the peaceful destination of many country road drivers. This haven just off Route 146 will reward you with several hours of worthwhile exploration. Harvey S. Ladew designed and developed Ladew Topiary Gardens to provide an array of plants that exhibit unique color, texture, and form for each season. He succeeded.

Twenty-two acres feature fifteen different themed flower gardens, ranging from a formal Rose Garden to a Cottage

Garden, Water Garden, and Berry Garden. Throughout the property, trees and shrubs are trained and pruned into ornamental shapes, making for a topiary fairy tale. The house contains English antiques and art and features a unique oval library. It's a beautiful place for wandering. There's even café dining in a picturesque barn or on the patio.

State 146 heads north to Madonna, where a right turn onto State 23 will lead you on a short two-mile trek before turning left onto State 165. The road leads through hilly farmland.

Following State 165, you will take a right turn onto State 24 south and continue several miles to Rocks State Park. This is a beautiful place to stop for a rest or to enjoy a quiet picnic. This scenic site features rock formations in the deep valley formed by Deer Creek. The popular King and Queen Seat formations, which can be reached by a trail from the park headquarters, make an ideal picnic spot. An old iron mill in the area once provided pig iron for the building of the *Monitor* during the Civil War.

After you enjoy a restful stop at Rocks State Park, get back on State 24 and head south toward Bel Air. You can either get on US 1 south for a brief drive before picking up State 147 or you can head into Bel Air for some exploration.

Bel Air is a small, friendly town. We stopped at the Red Fox Restaurant at 29 South Main Street, where we enjoyed talking with nice people and eating great seafood—the large crab cakes were some of the best we've had in Maryland. Bel Air features typical small-town streets. History buffs will want to stop to tour the Hays House Museum (1783), the Tudor Hall Museum (1800s), and Liriodendron (Kelly Mansion, 1898). If you decide to spend the night, we suggest you try Tudor Hall, the ancestral home of the Booths, an American theatrical family whose members included Edwin Thomas and John Wilkes, the assassin of President Abraham Lincoln.

Harford Road (State 147) heads back to Baltimore, but Gunpowder Falls State Park is a great place to stop along the way. This large park offers many activities and sightseeing opportunities. Gunpowder River was formed by the Big and Little Gunpowder Rivers, and the "falls" indicates that the rivers cross the fall line between the piedmont and tidewater areas. There aren't any actual waterfalls. Along with excellent fishing, tubing, biking, and hiking opportunities, Gunpowder Falls State Park features lots of history.

As you leave the park turn left onto Sunshine Road toward Upper Falls and go until you reach Kingsville. St. John's Episcopal Church in Kingsville is actually the combination of two churches: a tiny chapel built in the 1800s and a large Gothic-style stone church (look for the historical marker at the front of the chapel).

Next turn left onto Jerusalem Road and stop at St. Paul's Lutheran Church, which has a beautiful old cemetery with tombstones marking the final resting places of many early Kingsville families. Stay on Jerusalem Road until you reach Little Gunpowder Falls and take a right onto Jericho Road.

This pretty country lane follows the turns of the river to the Jericho Covered Bridge, a rebuilt wooden bridge, first erected in the mid-1800s, which spans eighty-eight feet over the river. On the other side of the bridge, you will see Jericho Farmhouse, a sturdy fieldstone building overlooking the river.

Just off the road, the Jerusalem Mill is an example of early American architecture. Built in 1772 by David Lee, a Quaker from Bucks County, Pennsylvania, the five-story mill, known as Lee's Merchant Mill until the 1870s, was one of the largest merchant gristmills in the region. From there, White Silk flour was shipped to Baltimore, the surrounding area, and eventually the rest of the world.

Jericho Road continues along the banks of the river, and you will enjoy some great river and mountain views all along the way. Take the time to stop to explore the massive boulders, old forests, and rolling river. Ahead, the town of Franklinville evokes the feeling of nineteenth-century living, with restored company mill houses giving the small town a quaint charm.

Turn right onto Franklinville Road and continue to the tiny village of Upper Falls. This town looks roughly the same as it did when the first train steamed into the station in the 1880s. Be sure to browse through the antique shop and wander the cemetery. You can then return to Harford Road by way of Bradshaw Road and Sunshine Avenue.

Harford Road (State 147) then runs through another small section of Gunpowder Falls State Park. Just after the park, look for a right turn onto Cub Hill Road. Then turn left onto Old Harford Road and right onto Proctor Lane.

All these turns are worth it when you pull into Weber's Cider Mill Farm at 2526 Proctor Lane. People come from throughout the Baltimore metropolitan area to this popular year-round farm. It has seasonal fruits and vegetables, events, children's activities, and much more. It's a delightful last stop on a Baltimore day trip.

Back on Harford Road, the Baltimore beltway looms just ahead, with urban and suburban commercial reminders all around. It's a far cry from the rest of a beautiful day away from the Baltimore hubbub.

In the Area

Towson Town Center (Towson): 410-494-8800

Hampton National Historic Site (Towson): 410-823-7054

Loch Raven Reservoir (Baltimore County): 410-252-3851

Ladew Topiary Gardens (Harford County): 410-557-9570

Rocks State Park (Harford County): 410-557-7994

Red Fox Restaurant (Bel Air): 410-879-3030

Hays House Museum (Bel Air): 410-879-1534

Tudor Hall Museum (Bel Air): 410-838-0466

Liriodendron (Kelly Mansion) (Bel Air): 410-838-3942

Tudor Hall (Bel Air): 410-838-0466

Gunpowder Falls State Park (Harford County): 410-592-2897

Weber's Cider Mill Farm (Cub Hill): 410-668-4488

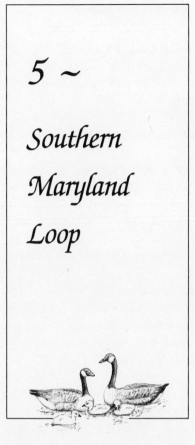

5 ~

Southern

Maryland

Loop

From Baltimore, take I-97 south to State 3 and US 301 south for the start of the drive in La Plata.

From Washington, D.C., take State 5 and US 301 south to La Plata for the start of the drive.

Highlights: *Tobacco farms and barns, the Chesapeake Bay, Patuxent River, Potomac River, Solomons Island, and historic St. Marys City. This drive is easily completed in a day, but take a weekend to enjoy the rural and water-oriented lifestyle of southern Maryland.*

Southern Maryland is just one-half hour from our nation's capital, but it's another world away from the city and the rest of Maryland. For lovers of the water and lots of history, this region makes for a great getaway.

Maryland was first settled in its southern reaches more than 350 years ago, when the first 140 settlers arrived at St. Clements Island on March 25, 1634. They came with the lofty purpose of building a new society based on the principles of religious toleration, separation of church and state, equal justice, and representative government.

In the land they called Maryland, settlers established a colony at St. Marys City, Maryland's first capital. St. Marys County was established in 1637, Calvert County followed in 1654, and Charles County in 1658.

The suburban sprawl of Washington, D.C., extends all the way out along US 301, but the quiet countryside is just a few miles off this highway lined with shopping centers, gas stations, and fast-food joints. Just turn left at La Plata onto State 6 to enter a very different part of Maryland. Except for fields of tobacco and tobacco barns, there's not much to see at first. Take a left onto State 231 at Simpson's Corner and head toward Hughesville. A Maryland Scenic Route begins west of Hughesville on State 231.

The crest of a hill provides a stunning view of the Patuxent River, before crossing over to Calvert County, "the Charm of the Chesapeake." In this tranquil tidewater peninsula you will find yourself in a charming time warp, where you can find prehistoric fossils, aspects of Chesapeake maritime heritage, and the energy technology of the twenty-first century.

State 231 leads right into Prince Frederick and the drive south through Calvert County on State 2/4. Another option is to take State 508 south to Bowens and then head east on State 506 for a look at Battle Creek Cypress Swamp Sanctuary. From here, it's easy to continue on State 506, before heading south.

Battle Creek Cypress Swamp Sanctuary is the northernmost naturally occurring stand of bald cypress trees in the U.S. This 100-acre nature sanctuary reveals a period 100,000 years ago, when large parts of the state were covered with swamps and saber-toothed tigers and mammoths roamed the landscape.

Today, walkers on the elevated quarter-mile boardwalk may see white-tailed deer, muskrats, opossum, pileated woodpeckers, and other wildlife. The nature center features many exhibits, demonstrations, and a unique observation beehive where you can peer inside the intricate world of the honeybee as nectar is turned into honey.

The road south through Calvert County leads between the Chesapeake Bay to the east and the Patuxent River to the west. This is a land ruled by the water.

Look for State 264 just outside Port Republic and turn right for a real education in the history of a one-room schoolhouse. Port Republic School Number Seven has stood for more than 100 years in a shady grove on the grounds of Christ Church.

Until 1932, one teacher taught reading, writing, and arithmetic to seven grades of boys and girls. At times, the classroom was so crowded that young students had to sit along the edge of the teacher's platform or in the aisles around the iron chunk stove in the center of the room.

Calvert County youths came from miles around to sit at the wooden desks, open their red and tan McGuffey Readers, and play recess games of Annie Over and Bug in the Gully. The schoolhouse was renovated and reopened in 1977 and welcomes visitors inside on Sunday afternoons and at other times by special arrangement by telephone.

An education in today's technology can be found just down the road at the Calvert Cliffs Nuclear Power Plant, near Lusby. This huge facility houses Maryland's only nuclear power plant and a unique visitors center. It's certainly an unusual thing to find at the end of a country road.

The visitors center, housed in a working tobacco barn that dates back to 1818, is filled with dioramas and animated exhibits that introduce visitors to the area and talk about energy and nuclear power. A stunning overlook provides a view of the sprawling power plant, which provides more than 50 percent of the electricity to Baltimore Gas and Electric customers.

On a clear day, you can see all the way across the Chesapeake Bay to Maryland's Eastern Shore.

Nearby, the subdued Flag Ponds Nature Park and Calvert Cliffs State Park both contrast with the quite active power plant. The 327-acre nature park features three miles of hiking trails, observation platforms overlooking two ponds, a wetlands boardwalk, a beach and fishing pier on Chesapeake Bay, and a visitors center with wildlife exhibits.

From about 1900 to 1955, this area was a sheltered harbor, with a major pound net fishery supplying croaker, trout, and herring to the Baltimore markets. Today, Buoy Hotel Number Two is the only remaining structure from that period and now houses an exhibit on the area's old-time fishing industry.

The highlight of the 1,460-acre Calvert Cliffs State Park is the view from Calvert Cliffs across the Chesapeake Bay. The cliffs were formed more than fifteen million years ago and contain more than 600 species of fossils. The view of the Chesapeake Bay horizon is just as awe-inspiring as when Capt. John Smith gazed out in 1608, when he named them Rickard's Cliffs.

Be sure to leave plenty of time to explore Solomons Island at the southern tip of Calvert County. Though it is quite busy with tourists, the area reveals much about southern Maryland and is definitely worth visiting in any season. Tiny Solomons is almost surrounded by water and features one of the world's deepest natural harbors. Its stunning seaport charm is worth much leisurely exploration.

State 2/4 leads right onto Solomons Island, where the modern Tourist Information Center is a good place to start and where you can find maps and ask for recommendations. You will probably be directed first to the Calvert Marine Museum across the street.

Drum Point Lighthouse at the Calvert Marine Museum

The Calvert Marine Museum is one of the state's top historical facilities. Through a creative mix of educational exhibits and programs, this museum provides an insight into the fascinating marine-related history of southern Maryland.

Visitors are immediately drawn to the Drum Point Lighthouse, one of only three remaining screwpile lights (cast-iron pilings were screwed into the earth) that served the Chesapeake Bay at the turn of the century. The charmingly restored cottage-style hexagonal lighthouse, which marked the entrance of the Patuxent River, was operational from 1883 to 1962.

The main exhibition building features a display of the fossils of Calvert Cliffs. Kids (and kids at heart) will love seeing the world as it existed more than ten million years ago, when shallow seas covered southern Maryland. This was a world inhabited by whales, porpoises, snails, and giant sharks. Remnants of these creatures are on view today in the museum displays, including the awesome open jaws of the extinct great white shark.

The museum's small craft exhibits will fascinate boat lovers and armchair sailors. Traditional Chesapeake Bay crafts are featured, including log canoes, a Potomac River dory boat, a Smith Island crab scrape, deadrise workboats, and skiffs for crabbing, sailing, rowing, or hunting railbirds.

Finally, the newest exhibition on maritime Patuxent tells the story of the people and changes along the river. The river has been used for transporting the tobacco crop to market, as a route to Washington, D.C., by the British during the War of 1812, and as a convenient travel route for yesterday's and today's watermen and tourists.

Outdoors, when you leave the museum, you find the peaceful estuary that features freshwater and saltwater marshes. The Chesapeake Bay and the Patuxent River come to life, and if you are quiet, you may see blue crabs, fiddler crabs, and green-backed herons along the banks of the river.

The rest of Solomons Island is just as fascinating. The town is perfect for leisurely strolling along the water, browsing through shops, and finding a delicious seafood meal.

"Old salt" shoppers will love Sandpiper Shops, Zahniser's Dry Dock Supply Company, and Island Trader Antiques. Book lovers can browse among 20,000 new, used, rare, and out-of-print books at Lazy Moon Book and Antiques Center.

On the food front, Chesapeake Bay restaurants offer some of the most delicious seafood in the country. We found many excellent dining possibilities, including Bowen's Inn (for good crab cakes), the Naughty Gull Restaurant and Pub (casual), and waterfront dining at the Captain's Table, the Dry Dock at Zahniser's, and Solomons Pier Restaurant and Lounge.

Overnight visitors also have many water-oriented options. Adina's Guest House offers a river view, Back Creek Inn Bed and Breakfast is surrounded by the water and lovely gardens, Davis House Bed and Breakfast is on the waterfront, and hosts Peter and Barbara Prentice at Webster House offer a quiet getaway (with a spa) a few blocks from the water.

The dizzying height of the Thomas Johnson Memorial Bridge adds excitement to your drive across the Patuxent River into St. Marys County. A right turn onto State 235 takes you into a land where, although much has changed since the first colonists arrived in 1634, still much of the landscape just off State 235 remains the same as when they first settled here.

Before venturing into the distant past, however, military mavens may want to stop by the Naval Air Test and Evaluation Museum in Lexington Park, a fascinating museum where you can view the results of the experimental work performed by researchers and engineers at the Patuxent Naval Air Test Center.

The parking area of the museum displays experimental aircraft from many eras, including a Loon from World War II and an A7 Corsair II. Inside, you may make a complete review of naval air technology.

State 235 continues south through St. Marys County, with the Potomac River just to the right and the Chesapeake Bay off to the left. It finally intersects with State 5 several miles from Point Lookout, where you can head back up through St. Marys County by turning right or continue down to Point Lookout by turning left.

Point Lookout State Park is definitely worth the detour. On the way, be sure to stop in Scotland at the monument commemorating the more than 20,000 Confederate prisoners who were held on this site at Camp Hoffman during the Civil War. It is the only federal memorial to Confederate soldiers in the country.

Just a mile down the road, the state park offers great views, hiking, biking, swimming, picnicking, boating, fishing, and camping. The visitors center features an excellent overview of Point Lookout's important strategic role in the Civil War.

State 5 leads back up the peninsula, with many interesting detours to tempt you along the way. You may be drawn to historic St. Marys City by many signs. Although the state has transformed it to be a bit like a theme park, St. Marys City still offers an authentic view of early America and Maryland's first statehouse.

Historic St. Marys City is a work in progress. Amateur historians and archaeologists will enjoy many things at this reconstruction of the seventeenth-century town. The 800-acre outdoor living-history museum is divided into four major exhibit areas.

The Brentland Farm Visitor Center features agricultural exhibits and an archaeology hall, while the Godiah Spray Tobacco Plantation depicts a working farm from the 1660s.

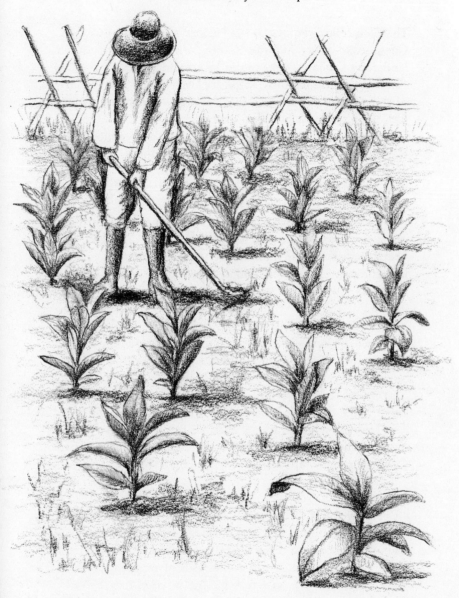

Hoeing tobacco at historic St. Mary's City

The Chancellor's Point Natural History Area is the site of the Chesapeake Indian Lifeways Center, where hikers can find a landscape similar to that found by the original settlers. The Governor's Field features a replica of Maryland's State House of 1676. This Jacobean building served as the state's capitol until 1694 and now houses a history museum. The *Maryland Dove* (a replica of one of the ships that brought the settlers from England) is moored in front of the State House. Farthing's Ordinary, a re-created seventeenth-century inn, rounds out the Governor's Field site and historic St. Marys City.

State 5 leads out of St. Marys City and right through pretty St. Marys College of Maryland. Founded in 1840, this liberal arts campus on the waterfront has an unusually charming academic atmosphere and is a great place to get out for a walk or a talk with some of the friendly students.

The Cecil Mill Historic District is the next stop on this magical Maryland history tour. Shoppers will love the Christmas Country Store, featuring handicrafts and original art by members of the Crafts Guild of St. Marys County. Located in Cecil's Old General Store (1806) on Indian Bridge Road in Great Mills, the store is across the street from The Old Mill. This renovated building now includes the original machinery used to run the water mill and the original sawmill. More than forty artists and craftspeople also have their work represented here at the mill.

A few miles farther on State 5, look for the St. Marys County Fairgrounds and The Farm Museum, which houses country memorabilia, from the tools of farmers, coopers, fishermen, and other trades, to the utensils of early farm life. As you step inside this austere building, an aura of yesteryear envelops you. You can almost hear the horses being harnessed or the chunking sound of butter being churned. The museum is officially open only during the county fair, the Oyster Festival, or by special arrangement, but it's worth a phone call to find out.

On the courthouse lawn in Leonardtown, visitors will find the Old Jail Museum. This building houses the headquarters for the St. Marys Historical Society and contains many county artifacts and historical records. One room is completely furnished as a "lady's cell" from 1857, and another features local physician Dr. Phillip Bean's office, furnished as he used it from 1914 to 1980.

If you have time, a worthwhile excursion will take you left onto State 234 just outside Leonardtown and left again onto State 242. Follow it all the way to the water at Coltons Point, which overlooks historic St. Clements Island and the landing site of the first Maryland colonists.

At Coltons Point, the St. Clements Island Potomac River Museum displays the history of the area, archaeological finds, examples of life on the Potomac River, and frequent programs relating to the culture and history of the area. It's a fascinating overview of life in southern Maryland.

The museum offers boat excursions to St. Clements Island. A forty-foot cross marks the landing where settlers held the first Roman Catholic mass in the English Colony of Maryland. The island hosts the Blessing of the Fleet on the last Sunday of every September.

State 234 continues back to US 301 and the end of the drive. The commercialism of this highway is a far cry from the country roads of southern Maryland that you left just a few miles behind.

In the Area

Battle Creek Cypress Swamp Sanctuary (Prince Frederick):
410-535-5327

Port Republic School Number Seven (Port Republic):
410-586-0232

Calvert Cliffs Nuclear Power Plant (Lusby): 410-260-4673

Flag Ponds Nature Park (Lusby): 410-535-5327

Calvert Cliffs State Park (Lusby): 410-888-1622

Calvert Marine Museum (Solomons Island): 410-326-2042

Sandpiper Shops (Solomons Island): 410-326-3008

Zahniser's Dry Dock Supply Company (Solomons Island):
410-326-2166

Island Trader Antiques (Solomons Island): 410-326-3582

Lazy Moon Book and Antiques Center (Solomons Island):
410-326-3720

Bowen's Inn (Solomons Island): 410-326-9814

Naughty Gull Restaurant and Pub (Solomons Island):
410-326-GULL

Captain's Table (Solomons Island): 410-326-2772

Dry Dock at Zahniser's (Solomons Island): 410-326-4817

Solomons Pier Restaurant and Lounge (Solomons Island):
410-326-2424

Adina's Guest House (Solomons Island): 410-326-4895

Back Creek Inn Bed and Breakfast (Solomons Island):
410-326-2022

Davis House Bed and Breakfast (Solomons Island):
410-326-4811

Webster House (Solomons Island): 410-326-0454

Naval Air Test and Evaluation Museum (Lexington Park):
410-863-7418

Point Lookout State Park (St. Marys County): 410-872-5688

Historic St. Marys City (St. Marys City): 410-862-0990

Christmas Country Store (Great Mills): 410-994-1170

The Old Mill (Great Mills): 410-475-2467

The Farm Museum (Leonardtown): 410-475-2467

Old Jail Museum (Leonardtown): 410-475-2467

St. Clements Island–Potomac River Museum (Colton):
    410-759-2222

6 ~

The Lower

Eastern

Shore

From Baltimore, take I-97 south to US 50/301 east into Annapolis for the start of the drive.

From Washington, D.C., take US 50/301 east into Annapolis for the start of the drive.

Highlights: *Annapolis, the lower Eastern Shore country-side, Kent Island, St. Michaels, Oxford, Cambridge, Easton, Salisbury, Ocean City, and Assateague Island National Seashore. This drive is easily completed in a day or two, but take your time to explore the unique Eastern Shore culture and countryside, staying in quaint accommodations along the way.*

The lower Eastern Shore has developed into a major Maryland tourist attraction, with much scenic beauty, colorful history, and the lure of the water. Yet, somehow, most of the region has remained a land of pleasant living (and driving).

Annapolis, the gateway to the Eastern Shore, is worth a quick one-day tour or a weekend stay. Although it's the state capital of Maryland, it still has a small-town feel.

Annapolis has been welcoming visitors by land and sea since 1649. This port city, sited on a convoluted piece of land where the Severn River flows into Chesapeake Bay, has seen seafarers, merchants, politicians, and travelers for more than 350 years. For nine months Annapolis was the capital of the United States during its infancy as a nation.

A walking tour of downtown Annapolis is easy and rewarding. You can follow the signs for Naval Academy parking and then take a shuttle bus, or try your luck with public parking right in the center of town. Good signage will help you to locate available parking.

The Victualling Warehouse Maritime Museum sits right on the waterfront and provides a great overview of the history of Annapolis. The highlight of a museum tour is definitely the large display depicting the Annapolis waterfront in 1751, when the city became the principal seaport of the upper Chesapeake Bay.

The vibrant waterfront area is packed with interesting shops, cafés, and restaurants. If you're looking for a place to enjoy a snack or a full meal, you'll find a lot of choice in the area. A few popular favorites include Buddy's Crabs and Ribs, Ram's Head Tavern (serving tasty microbrewery beers), and Middleton Tavern.

Middleton Tavern is representative of the history that pervades everything in Annapolis, including its food and drink. Like most eighteenth-century taverns, Middleton Tavern provided meals and lodging, and it also served as a link in the local communication network and social center for the region. The inn, originally opened in 1750 as a refuge for seagoing men, was run by Horatio Middleton, a ferryboat operator. His son, Samuel, operated the tavern, the ferry, and overseas trade and shipbuilding companies. He evidently enjoyed his own food and drink, as this poem written about his escapades indicates: "Eye shut, and mouth open, he loudly did snore, his arse on one chair and his legs on two more, and around him were strew'd many bottles and glasses."

Today, Middleton Tavern is still a busy refuge, for a wide variety of people working or visiting this popular section of

State House, Annapolis

Annapolis. The restaurant serves excellent seafood and its own delicious beer—just as Samuel Middleton would have liked.

Continue your tour on foot, heading up toward State Circle. The imposing hilltop-perched Maryland State House, the oldest one in continuous legislative use in the U.S, offers an interesting twenty-minute guided tour.

The Governor's Mansion at State Circle and School Street has seven rooms open for public viewing. The stately antiques-filled mansion still serves as the home for Maryland's governor. St. John's College, the third oldest school in the U.S., is just down the street. This liberal arts school was founded in 1784. McDowell Hall was built in 1740, while the "Liberty Tree" on the campus is more that 400 years old.

The Old Treasury Building, also on State Circle, now houses the Historic Annapolis Foundation Tour Office, which provides an array of excellent tours and programs. If you have the time, this organization is well worth contacting.

King George Street leads past many historic houses of note (Hammond-Harwood House and Chase-Lloyd House) and takes you onto the grounds of the U.S. Naval Academy through Gate No. 3. Founded in 1845, this legendary school has trained many of the nation's naval officers. Visitors are typically allowed in the museum, the chapel (look for the crypt of John Paul Jones), and Bancroft Hall dormitory (the sample midshipman's room is stark). Well-run tours can be arranged at Ricketts Hall near Gate No. 1.

The walk leads back to the waterfront by way of the William Paca House. If you visit one historic home in Annapolis, make it the Paca place, one of the city's largest, best-restored, and most significant mansions. This elegant Georgian mansion was the home of William Paca, a three-term Maryland governor and a signer of the Declaration of Independence.

If you have time, the waterfront area is a pleasant place to explore. The City Market House, originally opened in 1858, offers fresh seafood and other fare in a festive counter-service atmosphere. Many beautiful boats tie up at the inner harbor dock, as they do also in Eastport, a historic and photogenic sailing port across Spa Creek.

If you want to test your sea legs, Annapolis is a great base. Chesapeake Marine Tours, located at the City Dock, offers a wide variety of boat tours around the area, ranging from forty minutes to 7.5 hours in length and heading in many interesting directions on the water. It's a refreshing and delightful way to explore the Chesapeake Bay.

If you decide to stay in Annapolis for the night, you can choose your accommodations from the many historic inns in the city and from several dozen bed and breakfasts. The best bet is to call the Historic Inns of Annapolis for specific recommendations; be sure to ask about the Maryland Inn, the Robert Johnson House, and the State House Inn.

Annapolis provides a tantalizing taste of the Chesapeake Bay, and the lower Eastern Shore provides a full meal. US 50/301 leads east from Annapolis and across the huge Bay Bridge to Kent Island before it takes you onto the Eastern Shore proper.

Kent Island was originally settled by Virginians in 1631, but it's now a Maryland marvel to visit. While you're in the area, you may want to venture south on State 8 for a quick stop at Matapeake State Park, where you will have a vantage point for viewing the Bay Bridge, or you may wish to amble even farther to Kentmorr Harbor for a look and a taste of Chesapeake Bay seafood.

Busy US 50/31 leads past incredible commercialism, which belies the slow-down calm of the country just ahead. However, shoppers will love some of the bargains you can find at the many outlet malls along the way. When US 50 and 301 split, continue on US 50 west.

For an intriguing diversion, take the right turn onto State 662 south and proceed to Wye, a tiny town graced by two of Maryland's important attractions. The giant Wye Oak, Maryland's official state tree and the largest white oak in the U.S, is 450 years old and has shaded many country road travelers over the centuries. The Old Wye Church is one of the oldest Episcopal churches in America.

Nearby, the Wye Mill ground flour for Washington's army at Valley Forge in 1778. Robert Morris, financier of the American Revolution, ordered the flour and paid 10,000

The 450-year-old Wye Oak

pounds sterling (the equivalent of about $50,000 today). The mill continues to grind cornmeal and whole wheat and buck-wheat flour for armies of tourists today. Its cookbook, *Wye Millers Grind*, contains more than 100 recipes. Leaving Wye, continue on State 662 south before turning right back onto US 50.

US 50 runs all the way across the Eastern Shore of Mary-land to the Atlantic Ocean at Ocean City. It's a busy highway and starkly contrasts with all the country roads that lie just miles away from the speeding cars. However, it's the best base for exploring many Eastern Shore towns all along its path.

The first diversion from US 50 comes quickly as you take State 322 south around Easton and then State 33 west to St. Michaels and one of the Eastern Shore's most enjoyable destinations. St. Michaels is a microcosm of the entire Eastern Shore. This port town features a subtle wealth of scenic beauty, boating, museums, shopping, dining, and accommodations.

St. Michaels, the oldest city in Talbot County, predates the founding of Colonial Maryland, in that Capt. William Claiborne traded here in 1634. The town and river derived their name from the Episcopal church established in 1677. However, the name of the river was changed to Miles because of the Quaker influence in the area and their dislike of saintly names.

Due to its location, St. Michaels developed into a major shipbuilding city and is thought to have been the place where the plans for the Baltimore clipper ship were conceived. The influence of the sea has been and still is quite important.

In 1813, St. Michaels became known as "The Town That Fooled the British." On a foggy night, the British attacked St. Michaels with an artillery barrage. But they aimed too high, because St. Michaels's citizens had placed lanterns in the treetops to fool them. Only one house was struck by a cannonball.

When Baltimore became a major port, St. Michaels's importance as a major commercial harbor declined. However, boatbuilding and seafood remained important. In the last two decades, tourism has become a major industry and it's easy to see why.

One of the major attractions for tourists is the Chesapeake Bay Maritime Museum, situated on eighteen acres along the waterfront at Navy Point. The exhibits include a boatbuilding shop, an aquarium, waterfowling, a watermen's village, Chesapeake Bay history, and a floating skipjack and bugeye.

The Hooper Strait Lighthouse was also moved to the museum in 1966 and celebrated its one-hundredth anniversary in 1979. You'll enjoy the overall view of St. Michaels from the top, as well as an insider's look at a lighthouse.

The rest of St. Michaels is steeped in history. Historic houses that you won't want to miss include the Tarr House (1667), the Amelia Welby House (named after the first poet laureate of Maryland), and the aforementioned "cannonball" house. The St. Mary's Square Museum, located on the original town green, features local memorabilia. Also on the square, the unusual Museum of Costume exhibits historic fashions reflecting early lifestyles.

For a delightfully different view of St. Michaels and the surrounding area, you can take a trip by water—it's just like a floating country road drive. There are several boat tour options available out of St. Michaels. The *Patriot*, a large vessel, offers popular narrated cruises along the Miles River, complete with lots of history and striking views. The more adventurous traveler might prefer chartered sailing cruises on the *Footloose* and the *Jayhawk*.

Chesapeake Bay Nature Cruises and Expeditions offers another interesting outing on the water. Robert and Alice Jane Lippson guide guests on customized nature tours aboard their boat, the *Odyssey*. Renowned marine biologists, the Lippsons are coauthors of a popular nature guidebook, *Life on the Chesapeake Bay*. Cruisers can explore many natural wonders of this phenomenal body of water, including anchoring in quiet coves, netting fish in shallow waters, bird-watching, traipsing through wetlands, and many other possibilities that only the Lippsons can provide.

Back in town, shopping is the next tourist attraction. At both Celebrate Maryland and Chesapeake Bay Outfitters, you'll find a diversity of Maryland country road souvenirs. Flamingo Flats is an unusual store that specializes in a huge variety of different sauces and spices. You can while away several hours browsing among many other tiny shops just awaiting discovery.

All of this sightseeing and shopping might make you hungry, and St. Michaels responds with a wide variety of restaurants. Creative and casually elegant dining is available at 208 Talbot. You'll find great seafood in most of the area's restaurants, but local favorites include the Crab Claw and the St. Michaels Crab House and Bar. If you want to belly up or chow down with the local watermen, head for Carpenter Street Saloon.

St. Michaels requires a stay of at least one night, and you'll delight at the variety of choices. If you want a break from the bed and breakfast scene without staying at a hotel, the St. Michaels Harbour Inn and Marina is the perfect choice. This quiet, modern facility of modest size has forty-six luxurious waterfront rooms and suites with marvelous views. Other amenities include a popular restaurant, a marina, an outdoor pool, and bike and boat rentals.

Bed and breakfasts are also a good bet in St. Michaels. Call the Kemp House Inn (Georgian), the Palmer House

(Colonial), and the Parsonage Inn (Victorian) to ask about their accommodations—they are all charming.

As part of the St. Michaels diversion, be sure to continue out State 33 all the way to the end at Tilghman Island. This little island at road's end is a seafood mecca and hosts the last working skipjack sailing fleet on the bay. Here you'll get a close look at the working side of the Eastern Shore.

On the way out to Tilghman Island, you'll find three additional overnight accommodations to consider: the up-scale Inn at Perry Cabin, the popular waterfront Wade's Point Inn on the Bay, and the quiet Inn at Christmas Farm (ask here about one of the wonderful rooms in the converted chapel).

It's tough to leave St. Michaels, but the rest of the Eastern Shore holds more marvels in store for those willing to turn onto a few country roads. Take State 33 right into Easton for another Eastern Shore history lesson.

The busy city of Easton, formerly the Colonial capital of the Eastern Shore, now serves as Talbot County's seat. The best place to start an exploration of this historic town is at the Historical Society of Talbot County at 25 South Washington Street. They offer a number of guided tours of furnished eighteenth- and nineteenth-century homes, the regional Academy of the Arts, their own museum shop, and many more points of interest in Easton. Highlights of a walking tour include the courthouse, several old hotels, and many ornate houses from other eras.

If you can plan a stop in Easton for the autumn, be sure to attend the Waterfowl Festival during the second weekend of November. During this world-renowned event, more than 500 of the most prestigious artisans of the region display the finest in wildlife art, carvings, duck stamps, photography, books, decoys, guns, and many exhibits and demonstrations.

Many people use Easton as a base for exploring this area of the Eastern Shore. Two very good reasons for staying are the Tidewater Inn, one of the state's finest hotels, and Bishop's House Bed and Breakfast. The latter has been lovingly restored and offers a variety of quaint rooms and plenty of Eastern Shore hospitality.

The restaurants in Easton also offer another reason to stay. If you want to splurge, head for the elegant yet casual Hunter's Tavern at the Tidewater Inn, where specialties include their world-famous snapper soup, Chef Raymond's award-winning crab cakes, and a bountiful seafood platter. Be sure to enjoy a drink before dinner in the Decoy Lounge. Three other more casual dining options in town are the Legal Spirits Pub (in the Avalon Theatre), the Washington Street Pub, and Bullbrier's Saloon (great bread pudding).

US 50 heads straight out of Easton and into the commercialized twentieth century, but it's easy to go back in time with just a turn off the highway. One route is following State 333 over to Oxford for a look at another classic Eastern Shore town.

Oxford is more of a residential town than a tourist town. Many of its residents make their living in boatbuilding or by harvesting a variety of the abundant seafood from its water (the Chesapeake Bay's seafood industry is in the midst of a major comeback).

This small town is packed with historic stops. The Oxford Museum specializes in nineteenth-century maritime history, as well as that of Oxford. The staff can give you ideas for a historical tour of the town.

Just down the street sits the dock for the Oxford-Bellevue Ferry, perhaps the oldest privately operated ferry in the country. Started in 1683, and in continuous service since 1836, the ferry provides a unique and convenient route between Oxford and the St. Michaels area.

If you want to immerse yourself in a typical Eastern Shore town, stay in Oxford for a few days at the Robert Morris Inn or the Oxford Inn. The Robert Morris Inn overlooks the Tred Avon River and features quiet rooms and famous seafood. Just up the street, the Oxford Inn combines bed and breakfast hospitality with great dining and a chance to mix with the friendly locals at Pope's Tavern.

Head back to US 50 and the twentieth century just long enough to enter another time warp in Cambridge. Cambridge sits right at the mouth of the Choptank River, the area that served as the main stage for much of James Michener's novel *Chesapeake*.

In this wonderful book about the Eastern Shore, Michener writes, "It was simply there, the indefinable river, now broad, now narrow, in this age turbulent, in that asleep, becoming a formidable stream and then a spacious bay and then the ocean itself, an unbroken chain with all parts so interrelated that it will exist forever . . ."

Michener's Eastern Shore still exists in cities like Cambridge. This historic haven was founded in 1686 and still has many of the original eighteenth- and nineteenth-century houses along High Street.

The Meredith House and Neild Museum explore the history of Dorchester County. The former provides a fascinating look at seven Maryland governors associated with the county, whereas the latter covers the agriculture, industry, and maritime history of the area. Just outside Cambridge, on State 343, the Dorchester Heritage Museum presents a detailed view of the county.

For "old salts," the Brannock Maritime Museum is a treasure trove. Visitors can explore the history of the Maryland Oyster Navy, early navigational instruments, ship models, local maritime memorabilia, and an excellent Chesapeake Bay library. One of many highlights of the museum is an exhibit on the USS *Chester*, which was bombed, torpedoed, strafed, and straddled thirty-seven times, but always returned her crew from battle.

If all this touring makes you thirsty, head for the Wild Goose Brewery and a unique Eastern Shore experience. This local microbrewery, a popular stop with beer drinkers thirsty for a good brew, offers an educational tour that tells you what to drink with steamed crabs.

Historic Cambridge has three nice accommodations in keeping with the history theme. Glasgow Inn, owned and operated by a wonderful woman named Louiselee Roche, dates from 1760 and features an authentic historic atmosphere for a night's lodging. Commodore's Cottage offers private cottages in a three-acre garden. The Oakley House was built in 1913, after Annie Oakley and her husband had toured the world with the Wild West Show and chose Cambridge as the place they wanted to live. It's now a wonderful place to stay for the night.

For those who want to explore an Eastern Shore wilderness area, head south from Cambridge on US 335 to Blackwater National Wildlife Refuge. This large preserve is populated with waterfowl, other birds, and lots of wildlife that give the alert traveler some unusual picture-taking opportunities. If you have time, take a hike on one of the short trails, or drive slowly along the 4.5-mile wildlife drive.

Back on US 50, you'll join the rushing cars heading toward the Atlantic Ocean. You'll see very little along the highway before you come to Salisbury, though there is a wonderful bed and breakfast in the small town of Vienna. The Tavern House, an authentically restored colonial tavern owned and operated by Harvey and Elise Altergott, is a wonderful place to enjoy a quiet stay in a tiny town along the Nanticoke River.

Salisbury is a convenient base for exploring the southernmost part of Maryland's Eastern Shore. From here, you'll find many small towns, quiet coast ports, several wildlife preserves and parks, and even some Chesapeake Bay islands evocative of another time.

Somerset County's seat, Princess Anne, is just fifteen minutes' drive from Salisbury. The Somerset County Tourism Office can provide a walking tour map of the historic district, as well as information about other outings in the county.

State 363, bordered by beautiful scenery, runs west to Deal Island. The country road passes through several small fishing towns and the Deal Island Wildlife Management Area on the way to Deal Island and Wenona.

State 361 leads west from US 13 south of Princess Anne to the small old towns of Manokin, Upper Fairmount, Fairmount, and Rumbley. Along with an inside look at Eastern Shore living, the Fairmount Academy, founded in 1839, provides an inside look at old-time Eastern Shore schooling.

Finally, State 413 leads south to Crisfield and a unique Maryland experience. Visitors love this seafood capital and enjoy the waterside lifestyle revolving around the oyster. The Crisfield Historical Museum provides a colorful overview of the history and development of Crisfield's seafood industry. You can taste the results at Main Street restaurants such as the Dockside Restaurant and Waterman's Inn.

Crisfield is also the departure point for one of the frequent ferries to Smith Island. Lying about twelve miles out in the Chesapeake Bay, Smith Island is the state's only inhabited island accessible only by boat. The frequent ferries carry interested visitors to explore the three small villages that make up Maryland's portion of the island (the southern tip is in

Virginia). It makes for a unique excursion before returning to the country roads on the mainland.

The drive continues west on US 50 and into Worcester County, Maryland's easternmost county and the only one facing the Atlantic Ocean. You have two distinct choices for destinations: the busy beach resort life of Ocean City or the quiet beach life of Assateague Island National Seashore.

Ocean City is a wonderful beach resort city for those who enjoy this type of vacation lifestyle (and there are many). It has everything a beach lover wants, including a wide variety of accommodations, many excellent restaurants, and lots of activities. If you opt for a few days of Ocean City fun, contact the Ocean City Visitors and Convention Bureau for further information.

A totally different kind of beach experience is available just a few miles south of Ocean City. Take State 611 south across Sinepuxent Bay to the Assateague Island National Seashore and a beach beyond belief. This island refuge is a perfect example of good government. Assateague Island is divided in half by the Maryland-Virginia state line. The Maryland half is a bit more developed, and the Virginia half is more primitive (but features the nearby town of Chincoteague). Another book in this series, *Country Roads of Virginia*, details a drive along the Eastern Shore of Virginia, ending at Chincoteague and Assateague Island.

From the entrance to Maryland's portion, at the Barrier Island Visitor Center, you will know that you have taken a route into a different world. This facility features exhibits, maps and other information, an aquarium, and park rangers and naturalists who can answer almost any question you may have.

From the marshes, through the sand dunes, to the beach and the Atlantic Ocean, Assateague Island is packed with wildlife for everyone to see and enjoy. The National Park Service offers many guided walks, talks, and programs that provide further insight into this wonderful world of waves, sand, birds, wild horses, and unique plants and animals.

If you want to spend the night in this paradise, you'll have to be a happy camper. The 680-acre Assateague State Park offers camping, with bathhouses, hot showers, a seasonal restaurant, and many activities. The National Park Service offers campgrounds oceanside and beachside, with primitive facilities for those roughing it.

To enjoy the Assateague experience in a little more comfort, stay in Ocean City or head for the quietly appropriate town of Snow Hill just to the south. Here, bed and breakfasts include Chanceford Hall, River House Inn, and Snow Hill Inn.

In the Area

Victualling Warehouse Maritime Museum (Annapolis): 410-268-5576

Buddy's Crabs and Ribs (Annapolis): 410-269-1800

Ram's Head Tavern (Annapolis): 410-268-4545

Middleton Tavern (Annapolis): 410-263-3323

Maryland State House (Annapolis): 410-974-3400

Governor's Mansion (Annapolis): 410-974-3531

St. John's College (Annapolis): 410-263-2371

Historic Annapolis Foundation Tour Office (Annapolis): 410-267-8149

Hammond-Harwood House (Annapolis): 410-269-1714

Chase-Lloyd House (Annapolis): 410-263-2723

U.S. Naval Academy (Annapolis): 410-263-6933

William Paca House (Annapolis): 410-263-5553

City Market House (Annapolis): 410-263-7940

Chesapeake Marine Tours (Annapolis): 410-268-7600

Historic Inns of Annapolis (Annapolis): 410-263-2641

Old Wye Church (Wye Mills): 410-827-8853

Wye Mill (Wye Mills): 410-827-6909

Chesapeake Bay Maritime Museum (St. Michaels):
410-745-2916

St. Mary's Square Museum (St. Michaels): 410-745-9561

Museum of Costume (St. Michaels): 410-745-5154

Patriot Cruises (St. Michaels): 410-745-3100

Footloose Sailing Charter (St. Michaels): 410-745-3717

Jayhawk Sailing (St. Michaels): 410-745-2911

Chesapeake Bay Nature Cruises and Expeditions
(St. Michaels): 410-745-3255

Celebrate Maryland (St. Michaels): 410-745-5900

Chesapeake Bay Outfitters (St. Michaels): 410-745-3107

Flamingo Flats (St. Michaels): 410-745-2053

208 Talbot (St. Michaels): 410-745-3838

Crab Claw (St. Michaels): 410-745-2900

St. Michaels Crab House and Bar (St. Michaels):
410-745-5954

Carpenter Street Saloon (St. Michaels): 410-745-5111

St. Michaels Harbour Inn and Marina (St. Michaels):
410-745-9001

Kemp House Inn (St. Michaels): 410-745-2243

Palmer House (St. Michaels): 410-745-3319

Parsonage Inn (St. Michaels): 410-745-5519

Inn at Perry Cabin (St. Michaels): 410-745-5178

Wade's Point Inn on the Bay (St. Michaels): 410-745-2500

Inn at Christmas Farm (St. Michaels): 410-822-4470

Historical Society of Talbot County (Easton): 410-822-0773

Tidewater Inn (Easton): 410-822-1300

Bishop's House Bed and Breakfast (Easton): 410-820-7290

Hunter's Tavern (Easton): 410-822-1300

Legal Spirits Pub (Easton): 410-822-5522

Washington Street Pub (Easton): 410-822-9011

Bullbrier's Saloon (Easton): 410-819-0055

Oxford-Bellevue Ferry (Oxford): 410-745-9023

Oxford Museum (Oxford): 410-226-5122

Robert Morris Inn (Oxford): 410-226-5111

Oxford Inn and Pope's Tavern (Oxford): 410-226-5220

Meredith House and Neild Museum (Cambridge): 410-228-7953

Dorchester Heritage Museum (Cambridge): 410-228-5530

Brannock Maritime Museum (Cambridge): 410-228-6938

Wild Goose Brewery (Cambridge): 410-221-1121

Glasgow Inn (Cambridge): 410-228-0575

Commodore's Cottage (Cambridge): 410-228-6938

Oakley House (Cambridge): 410-228-6623

Blackwater National Wildlife Refuge (Dorchester County): 410-228-2677

Tavern House (Vienna): 410-376-3347

Somerset County Tourism Office (Princess Anne): 410-651-2968

Fairmount Academy (Upper Fairmount): 410-651-0351

Crisfield Historical Museum (Crisfield): 410-968-2501

Dockside Restaurant (Crisfield): 410-968-0111

Waterman's Inn (Crisfield): 410-968-2119

Smith Island (Chesapeake Bay): 410-651-2968

Ocean City Visitors and Convention Bureau (Ocean City):
410-289-8181

Assateague Island National Seashore (Assateague Island):
410-641-1441

Assateague State Park (Assateague Island): 410-641-2120

Barrier Island Visitors Center (Assateague Island):
410-641-3030

Chanceford Hall (Snow Hill): 410-632-2231

River House Inn (Snow Hill): 410-632-2772

Snow Hill Inn (Snow Hill): 410-632-2102

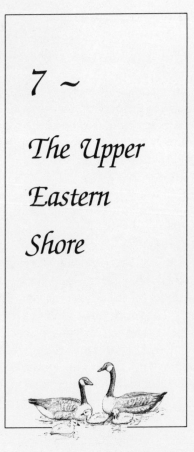

7 ~

The Upper

Eastern

Shore

From Baltimore, take I-97 south to US 50/301 east into Annapolis for the start of the drive. The drive could also be completed in reverse, by starting in Havre de Grace. Take I-95 north to State 155 east for the start of the drive.

From Washington, D.C., take US 50/301 east into Annapolis for the start of the drive. The drive could also be completed in reverse, by starting in Havre de Grace. Take I-95 north to State 155 east for the start of the drive.

Highlights: *Annapolis (see Chapter 6), the upper Eastern Shore countryside, Centreville, Chestertown, Rock Hall, Chesapeake City, Elkton, North East, Havre de Grace. This drive is easily completed in two days, but take your time to explore the unique Eastern Shore culture and countryside, staying in quaint accommodations along the way.*

The upper Chesapeake Bay defines life along the upper Eastern Shore. Towns (and tourism) are ruled by the ways of bay living—rules that are fun to follow.

The gateway to the Eastern Shore is Annapolis, which is fun to explore for a day or more, before heading across the Chesapeake Bay. This town is steeped in the history of Maryland and the water (see details in Chapter 6).

US 50/301 leads across the Chesapeake Bay, with too much typical commercialism lining the highway. The only salvations are a number of excellent places to stop for crabs and other seafood. Just look for signs advertising "Steamed Crabs" along the way.

A world far away from the commercial clutter and outlet shopping centers is just off the busy road, only five miles past the bridge. State 213 (a marked Scenic Route) leads all the way north, providing a perfect country road to explore the upper Eastern Shore.

Just five miles north of US 50/301, Centreville gives a tantalizing taste of Eastern Shore touring. This historically important town is the county seat of Queen Annes County and is a great place to stop for the day (and night).

Queen Annes County was founded by the Maryland General Assembly in 1706, which called for the establishment of a town at Coursey's Creek just off the Chester River and named it Queen Anne's Town. The courthouse, built in 1708, still serves as Queenstown's town hall and meeting place.

Queenstown was an active trading post and county seat until the end of the Revolutionary War, when a new town was established in 1782 near the Corsica River. A new courthouse was built there in 1792, and it subsequently became the town center of Centreville.

This 1792 Court House, still in use today, is thought to be the oldest county courthouse in continuous use in Maryland. It sits on the pretty town green, where a photogenic statue of Queen Anne was dedicated by Princess Anne in 1977. The southern side of the square features a row of eighteenth- and nineteenth-century houses that now make up the active offices of Lawyer's Row.

Many of Centreville's homes are steeped in history. In the 100 block of South Commerce Street, Wright's Chance and the Tucker House are houses definitely worth visiting. Both homes were built in the eighteenth century and were typical Eastern Shore houses.

Wright's Chance, built on farmland in 1744 and furnished with period antiques, was moved into town and now serves as the Queen Annes County Historical Society headquarters. Tucker House, built in 1794, serves as the society's museum for county and state history. Both are Eastern Shore history havens.

You'll enjoy a stop to spend the night amidst the history of Centreville, where in the center of town you'll find the Rose Tree Bed and Breakfast. This old house was originally built in 1790, but now has many different additions. Suzanne and Oliver James are the helpful hosts at this quaint small-town inn.

For a taste of nineteenth century Eastern Shore living, head for Locust Hill Bed and Breakfast. This pre–Revolutionary War farm estate has been in the Turpin family since 1812, and guests can now enjoy these historic surroundings and the family's hospitality. Ann and William Turpin are wonderful Centreville hosts in their private residence, making your stay feel like a visit to old Eastern Shore friends. The rooms are lovely and comfortable, and you'll enjoy the charming formal garden, a hearty continental breakfast, and lots of Eastern Shore touring and dining tips from the Turpins.

An eight-mile drive farther north brings you to Church Hill, a town that developed around St. Luke's Episcopal Church, for which it was named. Notice the stunning gambrel roof on this pretty church, built in 1732 with bricks imported from England. Inside, look for the tablets containing the Ten Commandments and the Lord's Prayer, which are said to be gifts from Queen Anne. A small nineteenth-century elementary school building is also on the grounds.

State 213 continues north across the Chester River Bridge and into Kent County and the historically phenomenal county seat, Chestertown. Because this city is packed with well-preserved history, you'll want to stay long enough to explore it well.

Founded in 1698, Chestertown became a thriving Chester River port town before the Revolutionary War. The results of this success can still be seen throughout the city today.

Starting from the town square, a walking tour of Chestertown is like stroll back into the eighteenth century. Stop at the Kent County Chamber of Commerce at 400 High Street to pick up a walking tour brochure.

The wealth of the early seafarers and merchants is evident in the character of the homes they built for themselves throughout Chestertown, many of which are on or near Water Street. Some of the highlights include Widehall (101 Water Street), an eighteenth-century merchant's home (now private); Nicholson House (111 Queen Street), the home of a Continental navy captain (private); and the Geddes-Piper House in Church Alley, a Philadelphia-style town house that now serves as the headquarters for the Kent County Historical Society.

At the corner of Front and Water streets, walkers will find the Customs House along the Chester River. Near this site, the townspeople staged their own anti-British "tea party" in 1774, supporting the actions of Bostonians to the north by boarding a brigantine and dumping tea into the river.

Even more history can be found within a few blocks. High Street is the hub of Chestertown's commercial activity, just as it has been for almost 300 years. You'll want to spend some time here browsing among the shops, window shopping, and enjoying the ambience of the area.

The White Swan Tavern at 231 High Street has been restored to its 1795 appearance and offers accommodations and enjoyable afternoon tea service. Just across the street sits the old Imperial Hotel, where you'll find a delicious meal and historical accommodations.

Farther up High Street look for the "Rock of Ages" house at number 532. This unusual home is said to have been built in the eighteenth century from the stone that the builder, Captain Palmer, brought over from England as ship's ballast.

Just outside the center of town is Washington College, on a quiet, spacious campus. This institution is the tenth oldest college in the nation and the only one to which George Washington personally granted the use of his name.

With so much to see, you may wish to find lodging in Chestertown, because it provides a convenient place for exploring the city and the rest of Kent County. Some good bed and breakfast choices include the Country Inn at Rolph's Wharf, Hill's Inn, and Widow's Walk Inn. Chestertown also features several excellent restaurants, including the Ironstone Cafe, the Newtowne Square Pub, the Old Wharf Inn, and the Imperial Dining Room.

An excursion to Rock Hall is definitely worth the diversion if you have time, and you may even decide to stay overnight or for the weekend if you really want to become immersed in the water-oriented life of the Eastern Shore. Take State 20 south and west out of Chestertown about twelve miles. Rock Hall is one of the few remaining Colonial watermen's villages left on the upper Eastern Shore. In addition to its renown for supplying the area with seafood, it is famed as the place Col. Tench Tilghman stopped on his way from Yorktown to Philadelphia bearing the news of Cornwallis's surrender. Legend has it that he arrived at a Rock Hall inn to change horses and rest, shouting, "A horse for the Congress! Cornwallis is taken!"

Today, travelers arrive to take in the view and a meal at one of the fine seafood restaurants. Highly recommended restaurants in Rock Hall include Fin, Fur, and Feather Inn, Swan Point Inn, and Waterman's Crab House.

Waterman of the Eastern Shore

History buffs will enjoy the Rock Hall Museum on Main Street, which exhibits an eclectic collection of miniature Chesapeake Bay workboats and other memorabilia. If you find that the town is just too delightful to tour well in a short visit, try to spend the night at the Black Duck, Little Neck Lodge, or Napley Green Country Inn.

Back on State 213 north, the road rolls quickly through farm country. Just before crossing the Sassafras River into

Cecil County, look for the Kitty Knight House on the left side in Georgetown, a bustling boating community.

Georgetown served as a major stop on the post road between Philadelphia and Annapolis. The town was almost completely destroyed during the War of 1812, but the Kitty Knight House was saved when Kitty convinced Admiral Cockburn to spare the house because a bedridden old lady was inside. It now serves as a popular country inn and a relaxing haven for road-weary country-road drivers.

Cecil County is another one of those Maryland regions that is quickly being discovered by travelers looking for quiet getaways and using it as a base for exploration of the upper Eastern Shore.

Cecil County, in Maryland's northeast corner, is known as "the wedge," where Delaware, Maryland, and Pennsylvania meet. Mason and Dixon's famous line, drawn in 1765, formed Cecil County's final northern and eastern borders, with the other boundaries defined by the shoreline.

The road (State 213) rolls through the farmland of Cecil County, across the Bohemia River, and into Chesapeake City. This historic city is one of the few remaining canal towns in the U.S., and South Chesapeake City is a National Historic District.

Chesapeake City is the western end of the Chesapeake and Delaware Canal, a large fourteen-mile canal system connecting the Chesapeake Bay with the Delaware River.

As early as the mid-1600s, people realized that a waterway across a narrow strip of land could save almost 300 miles on the water routes between Philadelphia and Baltimore. Although tentative plans were made earlier, it wasn't until 1802 that the Chesapeake and Delaware Canal Company was actually formed, and construction of the canal finally began in 1824. More than 2,600 men dug and hauled dirt from the ditch for several years. Many Irish and African-American laborers worked with pick and shovel for an average daily wage of seventy-five cents. The canal cost about $2.25 million, making it one of the most expensive canal projects of its era.

The C&D Canal finally opened in 1829. Teams of mules and horses towed freight and passenger ships, as well as other boats, through the canal. Traffic peaked in 1872, with more than 1.3 million tons of cargo passing through the canal.

The project faced many problems over the years, including water losses, railroad competition, and ships too large to pass through safely. The U.S. government finally purchased the canal in 1919 and assigned its management to the Corps of Engineers. Over many years, the canal was improved and widened. The current canal is immense, 450 feet wide and 35 feet deep. Now a modern, electronically controlled commercial waterway, it is one of the world's busiest canals.

A ship transit of the canal is no easy task, because strong currents and bad weather can cause navigation problems. Many ships use pilots from the Delaware River and Bay area or from Maryland pilots' associations. Pilots, who typically board the ships as they pass Lewes, Delaware, on entering Delaware Bay, guide the vessel up the river and into the canal to Chesapeake City. A Maryland pilot then boards the ship and guides it into the Chesapeake Bay to Baltimore or Annapolis. Chesapeake City is the site of the "changing of the pilots." A pilot launch maneuvers alongside the vessel, and, without stopping, it slows just enough to allow the two pilots to switch places.

The Corps of Engineers maintains the old lock pumphouse in Chesapeake City as the C&D Canal Museum. You'll want to stop to see the fascinating pictorial history and many exhibits concerning the canal. A huge waterwheel, built in 1837, is one of the highlights of the museum. This wooden wheel used buckets to change the level of the water in the locks at a rate of 1,200,000 gallons an hour. The giant old steam engines used for power can also be viewed. Outside the museum, a sign overlooking the canal marks the midway point between the two bodies of water.

The small town of Chesapeake City is an enjoyable place to shop and stroll among many antique shops and specialty stores along Bohemia Avenue.

If you're looking for a historic meal along the canal, try the Bayard House, the Dockside Yacht Club, Schaefer's Canal House, or The Tap Room. They all specialize in great views, atmosphere, and seafood.

The Inn at the Canal, Schaefer's Canal House, and Blue Max Bed and Breakfast also welcome canal buffs for the night. The Inn at the Canal is known locally as the Brady-Rees House. The Bradys owned and operated many of the tugboats that traveled the canal. Mary and Al Ioppolo are now the proud owners and operators of the elegant nineteenth-century bed and breakfast. Just down the street, the former home of renowned author Jack Hunter, who wrote *The Blue Max*, is now a quaint seven-room inn.

A short five miles away on State 213 you'll find the town of Elkton and more Eastern Shore lore. Elkton is interesting for a quick visit, but there are probably more scenic towns to target for an overnight stay.

The Historical Society of Cecil County is located along Main Street in a pretty nineteenth-century residential building. The museum can be seen only by appointment, but it does offer many interesting Eastern Shore exhibits. Four permanent exhibits and regularly changing displays highlight many aspects of Cecil County's history, ranging from Colonial furnishings to Victorian dollhouses. The country store and Early American kitchen displays are authentic and interesting. Other museum holdings include the Sheriff John F. DeWitt Military Museum and the Reverend William Duke's Log House.

Another interesting shopping place in Elkton is the Sinking Springs Herb Farm. Located just a few miles outside Elkton (call for directions), this 130-acre farm invites you to explore an eighteenth-century provincial plantation log house and beautiful gardens and grounds (there's a sycamore tree that sprouted in 1578). As part of a 2.5-hour program, guests enjoy an herbal luncheon of fresh unprocessed food prepared with herbs and served in the old house.

Hosts Ann and Bill Stubbs provide this leisurely and relaxing experience, where a typical meal may include breast of chicken on homemade English muffin, topped with a mushroom and herb sauce; a fresh garden salad with French tarragon dressing; fresh garden vegetables flavored with herbs; and homemade lemon-verbena cake, accented with raspberry sauce.

Although busy US 40 is the best way to head west across to Havre de Grace, there are many quiet stops along the way. The town of North East and the North Bay Bed and Breakfast should be included if at all possible.

North East, a charming and historic town under the influence of the Northeast River, invites you to get out of the car to explore, and a new walking brochure (available in many stores) makes the history easy to explore.

North East developed when the British-owned Principio Company established an ironworks, called North East Forge, in 1735. George Washington's father and brother owned interests in the company, and after it was confiscated from the British in 1780, it stayed open until 1898.

North East's growth, although slow since then, has been greatly helped by the renewed interest in its history and lifestyle. The walking tour brings you to an old town lockup, a Colonial-style log home, the Day Basket Factory (in operation by the Day family since 1875), an early mill house (now the Mill House Bed and Breakfast), and many other historic buildings. The Upper Bay Museum features an extensive collection of hunting, boating, and fishing artifacts native to the Chesapeake Bay.

Nearby Elk Neck State Park is also a refreshing place to stroll. The varied topography at this pretty park allows hikers to go from sandy beaches and marshlands to heavily wooded bluffs rising more than 100 feet over the Northeast River.

However, one of the best reasons to come to North East is the North Bay Bed and Breakfast, a wonderful waterfront house that hosts guests for an unusual and enjoyable Eastern Shore experience. Thanks to hosts Pam and Bob Appleton, North Bay guests feel welcome to relax by the water or on the porch. Those who stay here may use it as a base for venturing into North East and the surrounding countryside. Because of the Appletons' fleet of power- and sailboats, North Bay is a great base for a sailing holiday and Bob is the perfect host on the water. Guests can take a sail and then stay on the boat (boat and breakfast) or choose from a number of half-day, full-day, and dinner/sunset cruises.

Area restaurant water shuttles, cocktail cruises, and cruise packages with other bed and breakfasts are also offered by Bob and Pam, who will also make reservations for guests at one of their favorite restaurants, Woody's Crab House in North East.

Well known as a sailing instructor, Bob also offers several instructional packages, and the calm waters of the area lend themselves to learning the art and craft of sailing.

Before rejoining US 40, take Philadelphia Road into Charlestown for a quick look. Charlestown was a busy port hub in the 1800s that declined quickly when Baltimore grew as a port and the county seat was moved to Elkton. Just as in modern times, many people moved to the big city and some even dismantled their homes and rebuilt them in their new locations. As a busy port and post road, Charlestown also had many taverns. Visitors can still see the Brick Mansion, the Queen Tavern, the Red Lyon Tavern, and the Tory House. The Tory house has been restored and now houses an exhibit and museum.

US 40 leads across the Susquehanna River and into our final (or first) Eastern Shore destination, Havre de Grace.

Havre de Grace is a quaint and charming destination for a day's visit or for a weekend stay. It's been popular since 1782, when a Frenchman in the Marquis de Lafayette party saw the shoreline and exclaimed, "Ah, c'est Le Havre, Le Havre de Grace!" It truly is a harbor of grace, with local tourism officials and many boaters calling it the capital of water sports on the upper Chesapeake.

On dry land, the Havre de Grace National Historic District is packed with historic homes and sites. Drive out to the Concord Point Lighthouse first and tour it and the Decoy Museum before driving back into town for a walking tour.

Built in 1827, the stunning lighthouse was one of only eight built by John Donahoo of Havre de Grace, and was part of an effort to improve navigation when the Chesapeake and Delaware Canal opened.

The Decoy Museum just down the street was originally a service building for the old Bayou Hotel nearby. The museum, dedicated to the preservation of the art of decoy making and the recognition of the area's "gunning" heritage, houses the complete collections of decoys made by Madison Mitchell, Charlie Joiner, Charlie Bryant, and several other famous artisans.

Back in the center of Havre de Grace, the walking tour takes you to many historic homes, churches, museums, shops, restaurants, and accommodations of interest. If you take the tour, you won't want to leave.

The Vandiver Inn and Spencer-Silver Mansion are two of the early stops along South Union Street, and they are also the day's final stop for many country road drivers. These huge historic homes now serve as popular historic places to eat and sleep in Havre de Grace.

Other structures worth a look (and a good picture) include Rodgers House (226 North Washington Street), the Victorian Seneca Mansion (Union and Pennington Streets), and St. John's Church (Union and Congress Streets). Your walk will also lead you past many interesting commercial establishments.

Up on Conesto Street, the Susquehanna Museum is located in the old lockhouse of the Susquehanna and Tidewater Canal. This canal traversed the forty-five miles between Havre de Grace and Wrightsville, Pennsylvania. Opened in 1839, the canal stayed in operation—at least partially—until 1900. The museum features the restored lockhouse, a pivot bridge, the canal lock and basin, and many historical artifacts.

Havre de Grace certainly serves as the logical start or finish to any exploration of the upper Eastern Shore.

In the Area

Queen Annes County Historical Society (Centreville): 410-758-2300

Rose Tree Bed and Breakfast (Centreville): 410-758-3991

Locust Hill Bed and Breakfast (Centreville): 410-758-2682

Kent County Chamber of Commerce (Chestertown): 410-778-0416

Geddes-Piper House (Chestertown): 410-778-3499

White Swan Tavern (Chestertown): 410-778-2300

The Imperial Hotel (Chestertown): 410-778-5000

Country Inn at Rolph's Wharf (Chestertown): 410-778-1988

Hill's Inn (Chestertown): 410-778-1926

Widow's Walk Inn (Chestertown): 410-778-6864

Ironstone Cafe (Chestertown): 410-778-0188

Newtowne Square Pub (Chestertown): 410-778-1984

Old Wharf Inn (Chestertown): 410-778-3566

Imperial Dining Room (Chestertown): 410-778-5000

Fin, Fur, and Feather Inn (Rock Hall): 410-639-7454

Swan Point Inn (Rock Hall): 410-639-2500

Waterman's Crab House (Rock Hall): 410-639-2261

Rock Hall Museum (Rock Hall): 410-639-7611

Black Duck (Rock Hall): 410-639-2478

Little Neck Lodge (Rock Hall): 410-639-7577

Napley Green Country Inn (Rock Hall): 410-639-2267

Kitty Knight House (Georgetown): 410-648-5777

Chesapeake and Delaware Canal (South Chesapeake City):
410-885-5621

Bayard House (Chesapeake City): 410-885-5040

Dockside Yacht Club (Chesapeake City): 410-885-5016

Schaefer's Canal House (Chesapeake City): 410-885-2200

The Tap Room (Chesapeake City): 410-885-2344

Inn at the Canal (Chesapeake City): 410-885-5995

Blue Max Bed and Breakfast (Chesapeake City):
410-885-2781

Historical Society of Cecil County Museum (Elkton):
410-398-1790

Sinking Springs Herb Farm (Elkton): 410-398-5566

Day Basket Factory (North East): 410-287-6100

Mill House Bed and Breakfast (North East): 410-287-3532

Upper Bay Museum (North East): 410-287-5718

Elk Neck State Park (North East): 410-287-5333

North Bay Bed and Breakfast (North East): 410-287-5948

Woody's Crab House (North East): 410-287-3541

Tory House (Charlestown): 410-287-8793

Concord Point Lighthouse (Havre de Grace): 410-939-1340

Decoy Museum (Havre de Grace): 410-939-2739

Vandiver Inn (Havre de Grace): 410-939-5200

Spencer-Silver Mansion (Havre de Grace): 410-939-1097

St. John's Church (Havre de Grace): 410-939-2107

Susquehanna Museum (Havre de Grace): 410-939-3303

DELAWARE

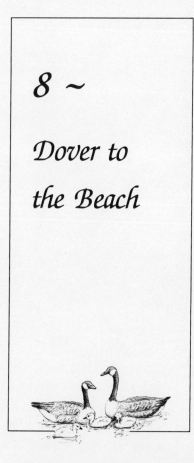

8 ~

Dover to
the Beach

From Dover, after exploring the city, take State 1 south toward Milford and Delaware's beaches.

Highlights: *Dover, Milford, Lewes, and the beaches of Delaware. This drive is easily completed in a day, but take a weekend and stay in Dover, Milford, or along the beach.*

If you like history, dive right into Dover. Delaware's capital is steeped in state and local history, all found within a short walk or drive of the city's center.

Downtown Dover revolves around the mechanics of politics, and you can while away many hours exploring the historic governmental buildings. Serious history buffs should contact the Dover Heritage Trail about their Old Dover Historic District and Victorian Dover Historic District walks.

The best place to start exploration of Dover (or the rest of the state) is the Delaware State Visitors Center behind the Old

Legislative Hall, Dover

State House at Duke of York and Federal Streets. This wonderful facility has helpful staff, many maps, lots of brochures, a gift shop, changing displays, and a slide show on Delaware State Museum sites. The Sewell C. Biggs Museum of American Decorative Art is upstairs. Its collections represent a variety of styles and periods from regional artists and masters of American art. One gallery is devoted to the works of Wilmington illustrator Frank Schoonover and another room is devoted entirely to watercolors.

The Old State House, a restored 1792 court/statehouse, contains an eighteenth-century courtroom and legislative chamber, as well as displays about legislative and judicial activities and how they impacted the lives of men, women, children, slaves, and free blacks of the area.

Across the street, beyond a shady expanse of green, is the Legislative Hall, which houses Delaware's General Assembly. The Senate and House of Representatives meet on the first floor, and the governor has offices on the second floor. Both floors are filled with paintings of former governors and Delaware's World War II heroes. The charming brick Delaware Supreme Court building is next door.

The Green is Dover's town square, laid out in 1722 in accordance with William Penn's orders of 1683. The site of early fairs and markets, it now hosts political rallies and public events, such as Old Dover Days in May, when many private homes and buildings are open to the public. The picturesque Kent County Courthouse, built in 1874, overlooks the Green.

Behind the Green, at State and Water Streets, sits Christ Episcopal Church. The stately church was built in 1734 and contains a graveyard monument to Delaware's Caesar Rodney, a signer of the Declaration of Independence.

To explore the rest of Dover's historic treasures, you may want to hop in your car. To continue in the Dover governmental spirit, head up to 151 Kings Highway and the governor's house, Woodburn. Built in 1791, this handsome Georgian residence has been the official governor's mansion since 1966, and although the house is open only on Saturday afternoons, the grounds are open daily.

Located in the former 1790 Presbyterian Church and 1880 Sunday School Building at 316 South Governor's Avenue are Meeting House Galleries I and II. These fascinating and well-presented museums feature 12,000 years of Delaware's archaeology and the "Main Street, Delaware" exhibit on small-town life.

Behind the museums you will find the unique Johnson Victrola Museum, which shows an extensive collection of phonographs, records, and memorabilia related to the Victor Talking Machine Company. E. R. Johnson, its founder, was born in Delaware.

Depending on the time of day you start your tour of Dover, you may want to end it by heading south to a country road, eating a meal, or finding a resting place for the night. Dover can accommodate all of these options.

Biddles Bed and Breakfast and Noble Guest House Bed and Breakfast, two popular choices in historic Dover, are both within walking distance of many small local restaurants.

After much historic city sightseeing, give your legs a rest and jump in the car for some quiet country road exploration. It doesn't take long to drive away from Dover's suburban commercialism on State 1. Military mavens may want to stop by Dover Air Force Base on the left just outside Dover, where the historical center displays a growing number of vintage aircraft and artifacts depicting air force life.

Just past the air force base, look for Kitts Hummock Road and the sign for John Dickinson Plantation on the right. This large reconstructed farm complex provides insight into life in Delaware in the 1700s.

The imposing mansion was built by John's father in 1740 and was one of the largest and most fashionable houses in the state. Along with the National Historic Landmark house, visitors can tour the reconstructed outbuilding complex, a log home, and the pretty Colonial Revival garden and grounds.

John Dickinson was one of America's founding fathers and is known as the "Penman of the Revolution" because of his many inspired essays on colonial rights and liberty. Of his plantation, he said, "Our place affords a luxuriant prospect of plenty . . . the clover lawns as green as a favorable season can make it . . . the trees bending down to the grass with fields of corn . . . and around the house as many turkeys and chickens [as] one would wish to see."

Beach lovers may want to head over to Bowers Beach on County 18. Set on Delaware Bay, this relatively quiet fishing village is a wonderful place to enjoy sun, surf, and sand. The Bowers Beach Maritime Museum at Main and Williams Streets in North Bowers Beach features many maritime artifacts, but it is open only on weekends during the summer.

Just north of Frederica sits Barratt's Chapel Museum and Archives on the right side of State 1. This Georgian-style chapel is known as the "Cradle of Methodism" because it was here on November 14, 1784, that Dr. Thomas Coke and Francis Asbury formulated plans for the organization of the Methodist Episcopal Church in America. The sacraments of communion and baptism were first administered here to the Methodists by John Wesley–ordained Methodist clergymen Dr. Thomas Coke and Rev. Richard Whatcoat. Tours are available Saturday and Sunday afternoons, as well as by appointment.

Before hitting the beach, you'll want to make Milford the next stop on the Delaware history tour. Historic Milford was founded in 1787, and a walking tour features an incredible twenty-nine houses listed on the National Register of Historic Places. One of these historic homes lured us there.

The Towers Bed and Breakfast Inn is a perfect destination for Delaware country road drivers. Innkeepers Sharon and Dan Bond will make any visit to the state even more special. The house was built in 1783 and was remodeled in 1891 in the rare Steamboat Gothic style. The Towers was once the residence of John Lofland, a popular early American poet and close friend of Edgar Allan Poe. It was later the home of Dr. William Burton, who as governor of Delaware sought unsuccessfully to keep the state out of the Civil War.

The house was carefully restored in the mid-1980s, opening its doors to lucky guests in 1988. Each of the spacious guest rooms is different in style and furnishings. The main floor features the popular Music Room, where guests tend to gather around the large fireplace, the 1899 Knabe grand piano, and the working Victrola.

The Towers features a spacious walled garden, a swimming pool, and a gazebo porch, where breakfast is served in pleasant weather. The Bonds provide bicycles for exploring town or the surrounding countryside.

If that's not enough to get you to drive into Milford, the historic Banking House Inn should be. As one of Delaware's leading restaurants, it's a wonderful accompaniment to a stay at The Towers.

State 1 leads out of Milford and toward Delaware's most popular beaches, passing within easy reach of the quiet Prime Hook National Wildlife Refuge. Here's another chance to explore Delaware's wilder side. You'll find two major hiking trails (including a boardwalk trail), as well as sandy spots at

Slaughter Beach, Fowler Beach, Primehook Beach, and Broad-
kill Beach.

The first stop along Delaware's coast should be the quaint
town of Lewes (pronounced "Lewis"), which is reached by
turning left on US 9. Situated on the Delaware Bay, rather
than the Atlantic Ocean, the town is known for its fishing
marinas, as the southern terminal of the Cape May–Lewes
Ferry between Delaware and New Jersey, and for its restored
historic richness.

Kings Highway leads into town and right to the Lewes
Chamber of Commerce and Visitors Bureau's information
center on the left. You'll want to park your car here, get a map,
and start a serious walking tour. The bureau is housed in the
Fisher-Martin House, a charming gambrel-roofed home built
in 1797.

Just down the street is the pretty Zwaanendael Museum,
built in 1931 by the state in memory of the ill-fated Dutch
settlement in 1631. Its exterior design was based on that of the
city hall in Hoorn, Holland, and the name means "Valley of
the Swans." Permanent and loaned exhibits trace the history
of Lewes and Delaware.

It's easy to wander the streets of Lewes. Front Street,
Second Street, and Third Street parallel each other, and all
feature historic homes, shops, inns, and restaurants. Some of
our favorites included Preservation Forge (a working blacksmith shop), the Old Fire House and Jail (not open to visitors),
and the Cannonball House Marine Museum. Second Street is
especially nice for shopping, offering Books by the Bay, Antique Corner, Kid's Ketch, Lewes Mercantile Antique Gallery,
and Pusey Weldin Antiques.

At the intersection of Ship Carpenter and Third Streets,
the Lewes Historical Society Complex represents an amazing
feat of reconstruction, involving a large number of restored

buildings that have been moved to this site. Guided and self-guided tours are available, in season. Most of the buildings date from the eighteenth century and include the Blacksmith Shop, the Doctor's Office, an early log cabin (Plank House), the Thompson Country Store, the Ellegood House (now a gift shop), the Burton-Ingram House (a museum of early Lewes furniture and portraits), the Rabbit's Ferry House (a fine arts gallery), and the Hiram R. Burton House (with a Delaware history reading room). Entrance to the complex also includes a visit to the Lightship Overfalls Museum, a seagoing lightship that used to be the Boston Light.

Lewes is a nice place to stay for a meal or for a night or two. We found two casual places for dining that we especially enjoyed: Gilligan's Bar and Grille and Lingo's Rose and Crown Restaurant and Pub.

Lewes abounds in inns. The waterfront Inn at Canal Square offers nineteen rooms in the main building, three rooms in the courtyard suites, and a one-of-a-kind two-bedroom houseboat. The New Devon Inn offers twenty-four rooms, two suites, and six retail shops. Other options include the Victorian Wild Swan, the new and interesting Blue Water House, and the Savannah Inn.

State 1 heads to the Atlantic shoreline and Delaware's twenty-five miles of coastal beaches and resort towns called the "quiet resorts." The name is relatively true during the summer and definitely true off-season.

Rehoboth Beach, the most developed part of the shoreline, is not included in the "quiet resorts" list, but it still retains the quaintness of a small beach resort. Rehoboth offers great shopping and a boardwalk from yesteryear. Since the 1870s, when it was a Methodist camp meeting site, it has been a popular destination resort. The Anna Hazard Museum, a camp meeting–era building, now houses the resort's museum at Martin's Lawn.

Along the shore

You'll find all kinds of small dining establishments right on the boardwalk, and if you're spending the night, you can choose one of the many modern hotels overlooking the beach.

Dewey Beach lies between the Atlantic Ocean and Rehoboth Bay just south of Rehoboth. This beach and water area is popular for all sorts of water sports. The adventurous may want to try the Millpond Paddler's sea kayak tours on Rehoboth Bay, Indian River Bay, Assawoman Bay, and other wildlife areas.

The drive down the shore presents many great pulloffs for the Delaware Seashore State Park. Large sand dunes separate the parking areas from the generally deserted beaches. It's a delightful retreat with beautiful areas for quiet walks on the beach, shell collecting, surf fishing, and picture taking. It's a beach lover's beach.

Bethany Beach features the next stretch of commercialism, but it's still pretty quiet. Here, you'll find a long list of places to stay and eat. Two overnight places with personality are Addy Sea Bed and Breakfast on Atlantic Avenue and Journey's End Guest House at 101 Parkwood Street. Our favorite spot for seafood was Mick and Mike's Crab House on Jefferson Bridge Road.

Fenwick Island features more of the same type of beach resorts, with the added bonus of the Fenwick Island Lighthouse, which began operation in 1859. State 1 then leads right into much busier Ocean City, Maryland. It's a far cry from the lovely country roads of Delaware.

In the Area

Dover Heritage Trail (Dover): 302-678-2040

Delaware State Visitors Center (Dover): 302-739-4266

Old State House (Dover): 302-739-4266

Legislative Hall (Dover): 302-739-5807

Delaware Supreme Court (Dover): 302-739-4155

The Green (Dover): 302-739-4266

Kent County Courthouse (Dover): 302-439-4266

Christ Episcopal Church (Dover): 302-734-5731

The Governor's House (Dover): 302-739-5656

Meeting House Galleries I and II (Dover): 302-739-4266

Johnson Victrola Museum (Dover): 302-739-4266

Biddles Bed and Breakfast (Dover): 302-736-1570

Noble Guest House Bed and Breakfast (Dover): 302-674-4084

Dover Air Force Base (Dover): 302-677-3376

John Dickinson Plantation (Dover): 302-739-3277

Bowers Beach Maritime Museum (Dover): 302-335-3462

Barratt's Chapel Museum and Archives (Frederica): 302-335-5544

Chamber of Commerce of Great Milford (Milford): 800-20-RELAX

The Towers Bed and Breakfast Inn (Milford): 302-422-3814

Banking House Inn (Milford): 302-422-5708

Prime Hook National Wildlife Refuge (Milton): 302-684-8419

Lewes Chamber of Commerce and Visitors Bureau (Lewes): 302-645-8073

Zwaanendael Museum (Lewes): 302-645-9418

Preservation Forge (Lewes): 302-645-7987

Cannonball House Marine Museum (Lewes): 302-645-8073

Lewes Historical Society Complex (Lewes): 302-645-7670

Gilligan's Bar and Grille (Lewes): 302-645-7866

Lingo's Rose and Crown Restaurant and Pub (Lewes): 302-645-2373

Inn at Canal Square (Lewes): 302-645-8499 or 800-222-7902

The New Devon Inn (Lewes): 302-645-6466 or 800-824-8754

Wild Swan (Lewes): 302-645-8550

Blue Water House (Lewes): 302-645-7832

Savannah Inn (Lewes): 302-645-5592

Anna Hazard Museum (Rehoboth Beach): 302-227-7097

Millpond Paddler (Millville): 302-539-2339

Delaware Seashore State Park (Sussex County): 302-227-2800

Addy Sea Bed and Breakfast (Bethany Beach): 302-539-3707

Journey's End Guest House (Bethany Beach): 302-539-9502

Mick and Mike's Crab House (Bethany Beach): 302-539-5384

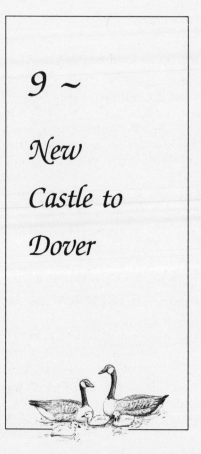

9 ~

New Castle to Dover

From Wilmington, take State 9 south out of downtown Wilmington for the start of the drive in New Castle.

Highlights: *New Castle, many wildlife areas, and Odessa. This drive is easily completed in a day, but New Castle deserves a stay of a night or more.*

Delaware's history is deep, and New Castle is a town steeped in state and national historical significance. Country roads in Delaware and all along the Eastern Seaboard lead to this undiscovered jewel of a town. Just park your car and put on your walking shoes, because New Castle is an inviting place to tour on foot.

New Castle, first founded by the Dutch on their way up the Delaware River, was later conquered by the Swedes and then by the British. William Penn first landed in North America at New Castle in 1682.

New Castle became the capital of the colony in 1704, served as the short-lived capital of Delaware in 1776, and grew into a vital stop on the north-south trading route. However, long-distance rail lines passed around New Castle and sent the town into a gradual decline. Through the intervening years, most of the buildings remained untouched and thus they survive today much as the Colonial and Federal generations knew them.

Today, cobblestone streets date from the Colonial period, as do the proud homes that line them. A detailed "New Castle Heritage Trail" map will guide you in a walking tour around town.

New Castle centers on the green, a good starting point for strollers. This common land, originally a pasture for the town's cows and sheep, was later developed into a pleasant park.

The New Castle Courthouse dates from 1732 and served as Delaware's colonial capitol and the meeting place of the State Assembly until 1777. The pretty cupola marked the center of the twelve-mile radial circle that formed Delaware's unusual curved northern boundary with Pennsylvania. Next door, the Old Town Hall and Markethouse marks the spot of the town's marketplace since 1655.

Walking down Market Street, you'll find the old Federal Arsenal, which provided ammunition storage for the War of 1812 and the Mexican War and later became a public school in the mid-1800s. The New Castle Inn Restaurant now occupies the building and you'll enjoy the early American decor, traditional and modern cuisine, and a tranquil setting.

Still on the green, you'll see Immanuel Episcopal Church, which was founded in 1689 and was the first Anglican parish in Delaware. Starting as a small structure, it quickly expanded. A fire in 1980 burned everything but the walls, which were used for complete reconstruction. The cemetery contains the graves of many prominent figures, including Delaware governors, senators, and signers of the Declaration of Independence.

Third Street features many old homes and public buildings, including the town's first private school (the Academy), the Old Library Museum, the Dutch House Museum, and the elegant Chancellor Kensey Johns House (private).

On Delaware Street you'll see examples of a range of building types and historical periods as you walk along toward the river. The street contains one of the most famous homes in New Castle (and perhaps Delaware), the Amstel House, built in 1738 as the home of Governor Van Dyke. George Washington attended the wedding of Van Dyke's daughter to Chancellor Johns in this home. The Amstel House Museum provides a glimpse into life in the eighteenth century, including a complete Colonial kitchen.

Delaware Street is also the home of The David Finney Inn, a respite for weary walkers who want to pause for a drink, to enjoy a meal, or to spend the night. The original innkeeper, Renere Vandercoolen, purchased the land in 1683 and built on it an inn in a town of "Dutch and Finns addicted to drunkeness," with accommodations described as "both mean and dear." The inn went through centuries of various uses and today serves as a living restoration of colonial atmosphere and history. Owners Tom and Janice Hagy, along with innkeeper Judith Piser, are wonderful New Castle hosts. Although no two rooms are alike, each bedroom and suite is furnished with period antiques and has a private bath. Each suite consists of a living room with a queen-size sofa bed, a large bathroom, and a bedroom with a king- or queen-size bed or twin beds.

The inn's gourmet kitchen serves creative cuisine in a dining room furnished with antiques or, weather permitting, out in the courtyard overlooking the formal gardens. The nautical decor in the inn's tavern overlooking the green reminds guests of colonial days when New Castle was a major sailing and shipping port. You will enjoy the exquisite ship models, original art, casual fare, and tasty draft New Castle beer imported from England.

Farther along Delaware Street you'll come to Cloud's Row. Designed as speculation housing in the early 1800s, the stacked design (one room per floor, three stories high) caused them to be called "band boxes."

Down along the Delaware River, walkers will find the New Castle–Frenchtown Railroad ticket office and the battery. The railroad, serviced by a steam locomotive (the Delaware), operated in the pre-Civil War period. Over along the battery, you can still see the earthwork terraces of early fortifications erected to control river traffic.

The Strand is lined with many fine homes along what was once New Castle's busy port. Inns, taverns, and even brothels were also once located along the picturesque street. The Great Fire of 1824 started at number 5 and swept up the Strand, destroying everything in its path until it reached the Read House.

The Van Leuvenigh House, home of the chief magistrate, was directly across from the water's edge. Number 6 and number 8 escaped the fire and had steps added to them when the street was lowered in the early 1800s. Number 8, the McWilliams House, is the oldest house on the Strand and displays a pent roof (a tiny eave) between its first and second floors.

Packet Alley once led down to the main public wharf of New Castle. Many important travelers passed through this alley on their way to Boston, New York, Philadelphia, Baltimore, Washington, and Alexandria.

Down the street, George Read II built the biggest house money could buy. With twenty-two rooms and 14,000 square feet, it was the largest house in Delaware at the time it was

New Castle

built. The historically correct restored gardens are the oldest surviving in the state.

To the left of the house is the site of George Read I's house. In addition to serving as acting governor of Delaware, chief justice, and the first senator from the state, he signed the Declaration of Independence and the U.S. Constitution. To the right of the house is the site of the Ship and Plow Tavern. George Read II ignored warnings about building his home next to this "den of iniquity."

Harmony Street will take you to a wide range of historical buildings and several centuries of architectural styles. The narrow front of the Immanuel Parish House on the Strand is deceiving, in that it stretches far up Harmony Street. Farther along, the small Rising Sun Tavern (now a private home) was one of the many eighteenth-century drinking establishments in town.

Second Street is the end of the walking tour that takes you back to the green. Armstrong's Row features speculation houses of the early 1800s that decrease in size as one walks down the street. Aull's Row contains simple and small wooden houses, again in graduated sizes.

A short walk takes you back to your car, and a short drive leads to another Delaware country road. State 9 wanders through scenic wildlife areas all the way to Dover.

Delaware City was conceived as a major Delaware River port and commercial center, which can be seen northwest of the town at the imposing Star Enterprise Refinery. The town center has retained much of its historic nineteenth-century atmosphere.

Fort Delaware State Park makes for an interesting diversion near Delaware City. A ten-minute boat ride to Pea Patch Island and the park aboard the *Delafort* leaves from the center of Delaware City. This Civil War–era prison fort includes a museum, an excellent audiovisual presentation, and a great observation town for bird-watchers looking for egrets, herons, and many other wading birds.

Just outside Delaware City on State 9, you will pass through Port Penn, typical of small towns along the river, where livelihoods revolve around the water. The Port Penn Interpretive Center offers exhibits on wildlife, fishing, trapping, and agriculture, a late-eighteenth-century small country store, and a schoolroom.

South of Delaware City, State 9 leads through low-lying coastal areas, including many wildlife refuges. It's a nature lover's dream drive, with many opportunities for using binoculars and cameras with long lenses. Bay View Beach and Woodland Beach also offer quiet and uncrowded Delaware Bay beach experiences.

History buffs may want to take State 299 up to Odessa. Odessa, known in the eighteenth century as Cantwell's Bridge, was a busy grain-shipping port. The historic district of Odessa offers a perfect example of restored rural American adaptations of urban Georgian architecture.

The four Historic Houses of Odessa, owned and operated by Winterthur Museum and Gardens (see chapter 10), allow you to imagine the village of Odessa as it once was. The Corbit-Sharp House contains regional and family furnishings that reflect life from 1774 to 1818. The Wilson-Warner House, built by prosperous merchant David Wilson in 1769, exemplifies Delaware Georgian architecture.

In a modern gallery setting, the Federal-style Brick Hotel Gallery houses "Nature Tamed: Belter Furniture, 1840–1860," the nation's largest collection of furniture manufactured by John Henry Belter. One of Delaware's oldest houses, the gambrel-roofed Collins-Sharp House, dates to the early eighteenth century.

Back on State 9, more wildlife areas await you on the road to Dover. Ducks may be a driver's only company along many of the stretches.

The town of Leipsic is another typical water-oriented village. Look for Sambo's Tavern on the water as you come into Leipsic, where you can enjoy cold drinks and fresh seafood in a local atmosphere.

State 9 becomes commercial as you near Dover. Though the memories are fresh from the country roads and towns to the north, this historic city is worth much exploration (see chapter 8).

In the Area

New Castle Visitors Bureau (New Castle): 800-758-1550

New Castle Courthouse (New Castle): 302-323-4453

The Newcastle Inn Restaurant (New Castle): 302-328-1798

Immanuel Episcopal Church (New Castle): 302-328-2413

Old Library Museum (New Castle): 302-322-2794

Dutch House Museum (New Castle): 302-322-2794

Amstel House Museum (New Castle): 302-322-2794

The David Finney Inn (New Castle): 302-322-6397

George Read II House and Gardens (New Castle): 302-322-8411

Fort Delaware State Park (Delaware City): 302-834-7941

Port Penn Interpretive Center (Port Penn): 302-324-0431

Historic Houses of Odessa (Odessa): 302-378-4069

Sambo's Tavern (Leipsic): 302-674-9724

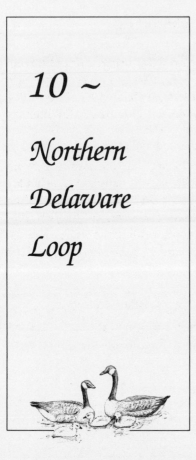

10 ~

Northern Delaware Loop

From Wilmington, take State 52 out of downtown Wilmington for the start of the drive.

Highlights: *The quiet rolling hills of the Brandywine Valley, the Delaware Art Museum, the Delaware Museum of Natural History, Winterthur, Centreville, Brandywine Creek State Park, the Hagley Museum, and Nemours. This drive is easily completed in a day.*

Northern Delaware is dominated by the skyline of Wilmington, the state's largest city. But country road lovers are only minutes away from small towns, elegant estates, and interesting museums nestled to the north in the quiet rolling hills of the Brandywine Valley.

State 52 leads right out of Wilmington and into another Delaware. On the way out of town, art aficionados should take time to explore the Delaware Art Museum. Follow State 52 (Pennsylvania Avenue) and then take a right on Bancroft Parkway. Follow Bancroft to Kentmere Parkway, turn left, and follow the signs to the museum.

106

The Delaware Art Museum is an urban cultural haven. The museum was originally established to house forty-eight treasured works by Howard Pyle, a Delaware painter called the father of American illustration and founder of the Brandywine school of painting.

Along with Pyle's works, the museum's extensive twentieth-century collection focuses on the work of Pyle's students, such as N. C. Wyeth, Frank Schoonover, Stanley Arthurs, Elizabeth Shippen Green, and Maxfield Parrish. The museum also has an excellent collection of English pre-Raphaelite art and many changing exhibitions and programs. It's worth the diversion from State 52 before heading into the Brandywine Valley.

Back on State 52, the scenery quickly changes to farmland and pretty countryside. The excellent signage throughout Delaware makes it easy to explore and find points of interest.

The first of these is the Delaware Museum of Natural History, just five miles west of Wilmington on the left. This museum offers varied exhibits ranging from local Delaware fauna to the wildlife of Mt. Kenya; a trip across Australia's Great Barrier Reef, an undersea world teeming with exotic marine creatures; and a twenty-seven-pound egg of the extinct elephant bird.

Less than a mile up the road, Winterthur is not quite as wild. Spread over almost 1,000 acres, Winterthur is an elaborate museum, garden, and library all in one beautiful setting. It's just off State 52, five miles west of the city, and well signed.

The information and museum tours office provides an introduction to touring Winterthur. General admission allows

visitors to tour the galleries and the gardens at their lei-
sure. The "Introduction to Winterthur" is a one-hour guided
tour of selected period rooms. The "Decorative Arts Tours"
include in-depth one- and two-hour guided tours of period
rooms.

Showcased in two buildings, the museum features American collector and horticulturist Henry Francis du Pont's
world-renowned collection of decorative arts made or used in
America from 1640 to 1860. The galleries include "Perspectives
on the Decorative Arts in Early America," artisan workshops,
more than 100 period rooms, a "Touch-It Room" for family
fun, and many more displays.

The garden is a lovely place for hours of wandering. You
will find beautiful vistas, quiet pools, and quaint corners
throughout the rolling estate in addition to thousands of
native and exotic plants in a lush setting.

The beauty of the Brandywine Valley continues as you go
back on the road. The small town of Centreville is just ahead
on State 52 and it's a great place for a rest stop. On the main
street, you'll find a quaint country store, many shops, several
art galleries, local restaurants, and even a town square.

From Centreville, it's just a mile or so to the Pennsylvania
state line. The best way to continue this Delaware country
road drive is to head into Pennsylvania before looping back
into Delaware on State 100.

State 52 runs through the quaint Pennsylvania village of
Fairville before intersecting with US 1. Take a right on US 1
and continue through the Hamorton Historic District (we
stopped at Chadd's Ford Winery for a taste of Brandywine
Valley wines). In Hamorton, take another right onto State 100
back toward Delaware.

This winding country road runs along the Brandywine
River through picture-postcard-like landscapes. Don't be sur-

prised to see landscape painters standing at their easels trying to put this beauty on canvas.

After passing through the quiet town of Montchanin, look for the turnoff to Brandywine Creek State Park. The rolling landscape teems with wildlife, including hawks, whitetail deer, a variety of songbirds, and elusive bog turtles in the freshwater marsh, Delaware's first dedicated nature preserve.

The park features twelve miles of trails for hikers, including the Tulip Tree Trail leading to 190-year-old tulip poplars. The year-round nature center offers a variety of programs, while the Brandywine River is a refreshing spot during hot summer months.

Back on State 100, two more elegant Brandywine Valley venues await. Take a right onto State 141 and follow the signs for the Hagley Museum.

The Hagley Museum was originally the du Pont mills, estate, and gardens. A visit provides a detailed look at nineteenth-century American life at home and work. The 238-acre site features exhibits tracing America's expansion from small water-powered mills to the industrial revolution; period actors depicting social, family, and labor activities; and Eleutherian Mills, the charming Georgian-style mansion that was the first du Pont family home.

Drivers who want to explore more of the du Ponts' lifestyle should follow State 141 farther to the Nemours mansion and gardens. Alfred I. du Pont named his 300-acre estate after the site of the du Pont ancestral home in north-central France. This overwhelming adaptation of a Louis XVI French chateau contains 102 rooms and is exquisitely furnished with antiques. The French-style gardens extend for one-third of a mile along the main vista from the house. Nemours may be

The Nemours mansion

viewed on a tour May through November, and visitors must be over sixteen years of age.

Back on State 100, the winding country road turns into Wilmington's urban sprawl. But the beautiful Brandywine Valley is still a vision in the rearview mirror.

In the Area

Delaware Art Museum (Wilmington): 302-571-9590

Delaware Museum of Natural History (Greenville): 302-658-9111

Winterthur (Winterthur): 302-888-4600

Brandywine Creek State Park (Wilmington):
302-577-3782

Hagley Museum (Wilmington): 302-658-2400

Nemours (Wilmington): 302-651-6912

Index